BOLD BOYS
IN MICHIGAN
HISTORY

GREAT LAKES BOOKS

A complete listing of the books in this series can
be found online at wsupress.wayne.edu

BOLD BOYS
IN MICHIGAN
HISTORY

Patricia Majher

Wayne State University Press
Detroit

ISBN 978-0-8143-4454-5 (paperback)
ISBN 978-0-8143-4455-2 (e-book)

Library of Congress Control Number: 2017953891

Wayne State University Press
Leonard N. Simons Building
4809 Woodward Avenue
Detroit, Michigan 48201-1309

Visit us online at wsupress.wayne.edu

To my stepson, Ben Chartier,
who has grown from a bold boy into
a multitalented and much-loved man

CONTENTS

INTRODUCTION

What inspires you? Praise from your mom or dad? An "atta-boy!" from your favorite coach? A high five from a friend?

How about a story that focuses on someone your age or a little older who did something really special? Would that inspire you to do something special, too?

In these pages, you'll meet a singer and a soldier, a builder and a botanist, a moviemaker and a machinist, a "wizard" and a world-class sprinter, plus a dozen other boys from all across Michigan who each did something amazing before turning twenty.

It wasn't always easy for these boys. Some grew up poor. Others fought against racism. Several had disabilities that could have derailed their dreams. Still, they were able to overcome these obstacles to reach their goals.

And you can, too—even if your goal is just to finish a math assignment you've been putting off or go a day without fighting with your brother or sister!

Start small. Then set bigger and bigger goals. And someday you, too, could be a "bold boy in Michigan history."

JIM ABBOTT

A Lefty from the Start
(1967–)

Jim Abbott didn't let his lack of a hand get in the way
of excelling at his favorite sport.

Mike Abbott drove fast to the hospital with his pregnant wife, Kathy, in pain in the back seat. She was in labor, and they were both rattled because their baby wasn't due for another two weeks. The couple barely made it to the hospital in time. After the quick delivery was through, the doctor found Mike in Kathy's room and shared the news with them. "You have a fine baby boy," he said. "But he was born without one of his hands."

At the beginning, raising James "Jim" Abbott would be no different than raising any other child. But the closer Jim got to starting school in his hometown of Flint, the more his parents worried about how he'd fit in. Not only was he lacking a right hand, his right arm was not as long or strong as his left. Jim's doctors decided that what he needed to get along in the world was a prosthesis: a man-made arm and hand.

The prosthesis fit over his right arm, then it was strapped to his body with a harness. It was heavy and hard for a little boy of five to use, so Jim was sent to a special hospital in Grand Rapids to learn how. He met many brave kids there, some who had tougher things to deal with. (One little girl didn't have any arms at all.) But he didn't like being away from his parents, and they didn't like being away from him. After a month, Mike and Kathy signed Jim out and brought him back home. The couple decided that the best way forward was to focus not on what Jim couldn't do but on what he *could*.

By the time Jim got to kindergarten, the "coulds" included working a fishing pole, riding a bike, and handling a baseball glove. But those skills didn't make up for the stares he got at school. Some kids were scared by the sight of the metal tongs that replaced his hand. Others teased him, calling him "Captain Hook," or asked rude questions. Either way, he didn't get what he most wanted from his classmates: acceptance.

In third grade, that began to turn around. That's the year he met a special teacher named Donn Clarkson. Clarkson had been born with weakness on his right side, and he had always walked with a limp. He understood Jim's challenges and did everything he could to help him overcome them.

It was also during that year that Jim competed against his classmates in a softball-throwing contest and won first place. "That was a huge deal for me," he wrote later in his autobiography. It made him feel like one of the guys. A little later came the day he talked his parents into letting him leave his prosthesis at home, for good.

At the end of elementary school, his family—now including a younger brother—moved to a new home. Wrapped around the ground floor was a brick wall. "There, out of sight, away from the world, I was free to dream," he explained. "With no one staring or judging, I'd stand in front of the brick wall, a rubber-coated ball in my left hand, my glove hooded over my right wrist, and I'd throw, and catch, and chase, and switch the glove back and forth." When he grew more comfortable, he'd move closer to the wall or throw the ball harder.

This drill gave him the confidence to try out for Little League. He got on a team and quickly made a name for himself there. When he was twelve, the *Flint Journal* sent out a reporter to write an article about him, focusing on his disability. But Jim let the man know that, even with just one hand, he could still reach for his dreams. "I look at major leaguers and I wish it was me," he said.

In Little League, Jim played third base and sometimes pitched. As a freshman at Flint Central, he pitched more but also played in the outfield. Sophomore year, he was promoted to the varsity team and locked in as a pitcher, moving on to win six games. By junior year, he'd become the team's "ace" (top pitcher) and led the Indians to the city championship. He also batted .367, with a grip that placed

*Jim Abbott, who was born without a right
hand, was drafted by the Toronto Blue Jays
at the age of 17.*

his left hand on top of the end of his right arm, which
rested above the bat's knob.

Senior year was when the college and pro scouts started
to show up to watch this young athlete in action. And they
were rewarded with Jim's best season yet; he won ten games,
hitting .427 (with seven homers) and helping the team take
home a countywide championship. The Toronto Blue Jays
were interested in Jim's talent, enough to pick him in the

thirty-sixth round of the 1985 draft. But the Central High School star had his heart set on going to college, at the University of Michigan.

Michigan's coach, Bud Middaugh, helped Jim throw harder and faster than ever before. Middaugh also taught the teenager how to handle the bunts that batters tried to sneak past him. The Wolverines finished the year on a high note, winning the Big Ten championship.

Jim's most eventful time in college came during his second season. In that period, the team won fifty-two games, including eleven pitched by Jim, as well as another conference championship. And Jim received one honor after another. First was the Golden Spikes Award, honoring the year's best amateur baseball player. Then came the Sullivan Award, for being the year's best amateur athlete of any sport. Jim broke new ground with that trophy; it had never been given to a baseball player before.

He was also named to the US team that played in both the Pan American Games and the 1988 Summer Olympics.

After He Turned Twenty

By the end of his last year at Michigan, Abbott had racked up twenty-six wins and eight losses. The California Angels were impressed by this record, and they used their first-round draft pick on the young Wolverine. He worked hard during spring training and made the team without playing a day in the **minor leagues**.

Abbott's first start was a major event. He lasted less than five innings and racked up a loss, but he left to a standing ovation from the huge crowd. He finally won in his third start, then settled down to pitch well for the rest of the season. He ended the year with twelve wins—the most by a pitcher in his first year since 1924.

The Angels finished the 1989 season in third place, and Abbott was voted the club's Rookie of the Year. His inspirational story made him a natural role model for kids with all kinds of disabilities.

Abbott had a tough second season, leading to a 10–14 won-lost record. Then he got off to a terrible start in 1991, throwing four straight losses to begin the season. After the All-Star Game break, though, he picked up steam; he ended up with an impressive 18–11 record and a 2.89 **earned run average**. Those stats earned him third place in the voting for the Cy Young Award, the highest pitching honor in the league.

In December 1991, Abbott married Dana Douty and waited for the new year to begin.

The 1992 season was a memorable one for the ballplayer, but for all the wrong reasons. For the first time in his pro career, Abbott was criticized for his play. Some people claimed that he had trouble holding runners on base and that his fielding was weak. (These challenges came from the unusual way his disability forced him to hold his mitt.)

Abbott's record that year wasn't great, so the Angels traded him to the New York Yankees for three minor

After retiring, Abbott was asked to throw out the first pitch at an Anaheim Angels game.

leaguers. The Yankees were hoping to make it into the play-offs, and they were buying up players with the best chance of getting them there.

One of the bright spots of the season was a no-hitter that Abbott pitched in the midst of a tight **pennant** race. But shortly after this, the Yankees' owner—who was known to be tough on his players—accused Abbott of not doing his job and spending too much time working with charities. This criticism angered the whole team, and they ended up finishing in second place.

Abbott's second season in New York came to a close in mid-August, when the players went on strike. At that point in time, his record was nine wins and eight losses. In December, the Yankees decided not to extend Abbott's contract for the 1995 season.

For the next couple of years, he bounced around between the Chicago White Sox, the California Angels, and the Milwaukee Brewers. After the 1999 season, he decided to retire with a career record of 87–108 and a 4.25 ERA.

On his website, Abbott talks about those numbers. "Some of you may know that my statistics weren't that great," he says. "There were some incredible highlights and some agonizing low lights. The truth is, I won't go to the Hall of Fame. But if a career can be measured by special moments, lessons learned and a connection with people, then I would stack mine up with anyone's."

Despite having to make his way in the world of sports with just one hand, Abbott says, "I was incredibly blessed in my life. More was given to me than was ever taken away."

Abbott, his wife, and two children now live in California. He has served as a pitching instructor during spring training for the Angels and makes his living as a motivational speaker. He also helps out in his community through Amigos de los Ninos, a group that raises money for children's charities.

In 2004, Jim Abbott was voted into the Michigan Sports Hall of Fame.

Sources

Abbott, Jim, and Tim Brown. *Imperfect: An Improbable Life.* New York: Ballantine Books, 2012.

"About Jim," Jim Abbott. Accessed November 27, 2016. www.jimabbott.net/index.html.

Bernotas, Bob. *Nothing to Prove: The Jim Abbott Story.* New York: Kodansha America, 1995.

Gomez, Isabel. "A Motivational Q&A with Former Pro Pitcher Jim Abbott." *Sports Illustrated Kids*, March 23, 2015.

ONE FINAL FACT

Though dedicated to baseball in high school, Jim also played quarterback as a senior, leading Flint Central to the state semifinals.

LIBERTY HYDE BAILEY JR.

The Boy Botanist
(1858–1954)

*Growing up around the apple orchards of southwest
Michigan prepared him to publish his first scientific
paper at fifteen.*

Liberty Hyde Bailey's parents were pioneers in the village
of South Haven on the Lake Michigan shoreline. Settling
there in the 1850s, they took advantage of land that had
been cleared of forests and began to plant an apple orchard.
Over time, Liberty's father became an expert in apples,
growing more than three hundred kinds in the sandy soil
of Michigan's "fruit belt."

South Haven was a wonderful place for a boy to grow
up. Young Liberty roamed the woods near his home, enjoying the world around him and taking an interest in his
father's business.

By his early teens, he had become an expert at grafting,
that is, attaching a twig or bud from one plant onto another

Liberty Hyde Bailey was already famous for his knowledge of apple growing when this childhood photo was taken.

so that the two grow together. (This is done to introduce qualities like better flavor or hardiness that the original plant doesn't possess.) This talent made him very popular with the other orchard owners, who paid him to improve their fruit. Liberty was invited to speak about grafting at the South Haven Pomological Society. (Pomology is the science of growing fruit.)

Though his greatest interest lay in plants, he also developed a love for animals. He once hatched snake eggs in his mother's oven. And he wrote a paper on birds, with a focus on saving endangered species. At age fifteen, he was asked to read his paper before the state pomological society. They thought so highly of his work that they published it in their annual report.

Around this time, Liberty began gathering samples of plants to study. Then, in a stroke of luck, a botanist (plant scientist) named Lucy Millington arrived in town. For the next two years, she helped to identify the plants Liberty collected and taught him the pronunciation of their Latin names. Years later, he would credit her for his lifelong love of research.

Millington challenged him to tackle the toughest subjects in botany, including marsh grasses. This sparked a research project that resulted in his second scientific paper. "I do not yet know why plants come out of the land or float in streams, or creep on rocks or roll from the sea," Liberty wrote. "[But] I am entranced by the mystery of them."

By the time Millington moved away, Liberty had grown quite confident in his abilities. He took the bold step of introducing himself to William Beal, the head of botany at Michigan Agricultural College (now Michigan State University), and inviting him to deliver a lecture in South Haven. Beal accepted the offer to speak and encouraged the young man to pursue his studies. Thrilled by Beal's remarks, Liberty began to take classes at Michigan State University (MSU) in 1878.

After He Turned Twenty

Liberty Bailey flourished at the university. Beal introduced him to all the great books about botany and then encouraged him to apply what he learned in the laboratory and out in the field. Bailey also continued to develop his writing skills. In his senior year, he helped launch a magazine that promoted scientific reading among students.

Bailey's ability to write helped him get his first job after graduation, at a newspaper in Illinois. But a better offer soon came his way, from the very best botanist in America: Asa Gray. Gray worked at Harvard University, and he needed help organizing his collection of plant samples. Bailey took the job, moving himself and his new wife, Annette, to Cambridge, Massachusetts, in 1883.

Bailey spent just two years there, but every day with Gray was like a new lesson in his favorite subject. It was also great preparation for the next step in his career: becoming a professor.

Bailey was offered a faculty position back at MSU, teaching classes in horticulture—the study of growing fruits, vegetables, and flowers. Some of his friends teased him, saying that horticulture was just a fancy term for gardening. But Bailey, having grown up in an apple orchard, ignored their comments and jumped into his new position with both feet. He became such a good teacher that students flocked to his classes. He earned a **master's degree**. He also found time to publish his first book, *Talks Afield: About Plants and the Science of Plants*. This led to requests to speak before groups in Michigan and beyond.

Toward the end of 1887, Bailey gave a series of lectures at Cornell University in Ithaca, New York. The series went over so well that he was offered the chance to lead

Bailey often traveled on plant-gathering trips around the world with his daughter Ethel by his side.

Cornell's Department of Horticulture. He was also given money to take an overseas trip to Europe.

In 1888, he moved his growing family—which now included daughter Sara—to Ithaca, the place where he ended up spending the rest of his life.

In addition to teaching classes, Bailey studied such subjects as growing plants in a brand new way: under electric lights. He also began to build a case for starting a college of agriculture at Cornell, as "a plain, earnest, and continuous effort to meet the needs of the people" who lived in the countryside surrounding the university. It took a while to convince his higher-ups. But the college finally opened in 1904. Bailey was named its first **dean**.

As dean, he approved courses that would help farmers better manage their land, their crops, and their money. He played a role in creating an **extension service** and 4-H clubs for children. And he was the first person to hire female professors at the university. As he explained, "The person who is best qualified to teach the subject should be the one who teaches it."

During this period, Bailey was also asked by President Theodore Roosevelt to head a national commission to study country life. The president was so impressed by Bailey's leadership that he suggested the professor run for governor!

After twenty-five years at Cornell, Liberty Hyde Bailey decided to step down. But he definitely did not *slow* down. In fact, one of the first things he did was to visit New Zealand on a speaking tour. On the long sea voyage, Bailey became inspired by the beauty of his surroundings. Thoughts came quickly to his mind, and he wrote them down on whatever paper was handy—even napkins. Once he got home, he turned those thoughts into *The Holy Earth*, a book about the environment that would influence many thinkers who came after him.

Bailey kept up a steady habit of writing books, papers, and articles in his later years. He served as the president of several scientific societies and was made a member of the **National Academy of Sciences**. He edited magazines on his favorite subjects. And he collected plants around the world with his second daughter, Ethel, by his side.

Bailey was planning a collecting trip to the Congo rainforest—at the age of ninety-two!—when he broke his thigh bone. His health declined soon after that, and he died at home on Christmas Day 1954.

The memory of Liberty Hyde Bailey and his influence on horticulture, agriculture, and education live on to this day in many ways. A classroom building and an **herbarium** at Cornell, a dormitory at MSU, and a community center and street in East Lansing, Michigan, all bear his name.

Sources

"About Bailey." Liberty Hyde Bailey Museum. Accessed October 12, 2016. libertyhydebailey.org/about/about-bailey.

Banks, Harlan P. *Liberty Hyde Bailey: 1858–1954*. Washington, D.C.: National Academy of Sciences, 1994.

"Liberty Hyde Bailey: A Man for All Seasons." Cornell University Library. Accessed October 12, 2016. rmc.library.cornell.edu/bailey/index.html.

Tolley, Kim. *The Science Education of American Girls: A Historical Perspective*. London: Routledge, 2002.

Places to Visit

Liberty Hyde Bailey is celebrated with his own museum, inside his childhood home at 903 S. Bailey Avenue in South Haven.

Two Michigan historical markers honor Bailey: one in South Haven outside his museum and the other in East Lansing outside Michigan State University's Harry J. Eustace Hall. Bailey designed the latter building, which is located on East Circle Drive.

Michigan State University is also the site of a statue of Bailey, which can be found in the Amien and Florence Carter Annual Trial Garden on Bogue Street.

ONE FINAL FACT

Liberty inherited his father's unusual name. Dana Bailey, father of Liberty Sr., had been an **abolitionist** in Vermont, and when he received word that his son had been born, he proclaimed, "Name him Liberty, for all shall be free!"

THOMAS EDISON

Bursting with Ideas
(1847–1931)

*His childhood interests in science and nature
inspired him to set up his first laboratory before
he even became a teen.*

He may have been born in Ohio, but Thomas Alva Edison, the greatest inventor of his time, spent his most important early years in Michigan.

Al, as his family liked to call him, moved to Port Huron with his father, mother, a brother, and two sisters in 1854, when he was seven. His father operated several businesses, but none of them was very successful. So Al pitched in and helped plant a vegetable garden, which he later harvested, selling the produce from door to door.

Al was homeschooled for most of his childhood. "My mother taught me how to read good books quickly and correctly," he later recalled. And read he would, tackling almost every subject under the sun. History, nature, and science were his favorites, and within science, he liked mechanics and chemistry best. The last topic inspired him to set up a laboratory in his family's cellar, where he and a friend experimented with dangerous chemicals. His mother was worried that the two boys would "blow [their] heads off"!

From one book, Al learned about Morse code—a system of using long and short sounds to send messages through telegraph wires. (This was in an age before telephones had been invented.) Fascinated by the idea, he made a device to tap out the sounds and connected it to a wire that he strung between his house and a neighbor's. This skill with Morse code would come in handy in his next activity: working for the railroad.

Al was thirteen when his father helped him get a job on the rail line that ran between Port Huron and Detroit. He became one of a group of boys who rode the train to sell newspapers, candy, and cigars to the commuters. The days were long—up to fourteen hours—but he enjoyed being his own boss. At one point, he used his spare time to run some experiments in the baggage car. That ended when a fire broke out. An angry conductor punished young Edison by cuffing him on the ear.

When the Civil War began in 1861, Al saw a sharp increase in his newspaper sales. The people of Michigan were very interested in what was happening to their boys down south. After the bloody battle of Shiloh, he saw crowds of people—desperate for news—gathered around one depot's bulletin board. He got the idea that if he telegraphed the

*Teenager Thomas Edison helped support his
family by selling newspapers and snacks on a
train that ran between Port Huron and Detroit.*

war's headlines ahead of the train arriving at a particular
stop, he might sell more papers there. So he talked a telegrapher into helping him.

His idea proved to be a good one; the commuters bought hundreds more than usual the first day. That
prompted Al—who was now calling himself "Tom"—to
think about becoming a telegraph operator.

He had some trouble getting people to take him seriously. Then, one day, he rescued the stationmaster's young
son when the boy stumbled onto the tracks into the path

of a train. As a gesture of thanks, the father agreed to teach Tom the telegrapher's trade.

Tom was a quick learner, and by age sixteen, he had gotten himself a job in the Port Huron office of a national company called Western Union. Later, he took jobs with the company in other cities and learned to tap out messages with more and more speed.

After He Turned Twenty

In 1868, when Edison was twenty-one, he moved to Boston, Massachusetts, to fill an opening at the Western Union office there. He worked hard all day to help people send telegrams. In the evenings, he worked to bring his ideas to life. One of his first inventions was an electric voting machine. But he couldn't find anyone to buy it. The machine was just too far ahead of its time.

He then vowed he would never make another invention unless he was sure people wanted it.

He began tinkering with an idea that would allow a telegraph operator to send more than one telegram at a time. When he ran out of money to finish the invention, he had to find some investors—businessmen who lent money in exchange for some of the profits if an idea made it to market. His search led him to New York City.

With the help of investors he found there, he soon opened a telegraph machine factory in the nearby state of New Jersey. He called his employees the "boys" and they called him the "old man," even though—at twenty-four—he was younger than many of them.

After six years, Edison grew tired of making things and decided to go back to inventing them. He pulled up roots and moved his wife Mary and their children twenty miles away to the small town of Menlo Park. The "boys" followed him.

Edison bought some land and began building a two-story laboratory. Later he added an office and library, a carpentry shop, a machine shop, a glass-blowing shed, and an engine house. He even had a boarding house built, where his employees could live.

He called Menlo Park his "invention factory" and busied himself and his workers with as many as forty projects at a time. He believed his complex was the perfect place to think. "The man who doesn't make up his mind to cultivate the habit of thinking cannot make the most of himself," he explained. "All progress, all success, springs from thinking."

Part of Edison's success came from being able to improve products that didn't work as well as their inventors had hoped. This was the case with the telephone. Alexander Graham Bell had designed this device, but it only worked over short distances and you had to shout into it to be heard. Edison's old employer, Western Union, asked him to look at the device and see if he could fix it. After giving it some thought, he placed two circles of lampblack (the black soot from an oil lamp) next to each other on the

Edison built a modern laboratory in Menlo Park,
New Jersey, where he and his employees conducted
countless experiments.

phone's **transmitter**. When they vibrated, the electrical current carried a strong, clear signal over the phone wire.

Not only did this fix the problem, it also paved the way for an original Edison invention: a way of recording and playing back a person's voice. He called it a "phonograph." Edison thought this might be a good machine for businesses, to help bosses dictate letters. But the bigger demand came from music lovers, who wanted to be able to buy recordings of their favorite songs and play them over and over. Edison modified the phonograph for their use. (This invention is the granddaddy of CD and DVD players.)

In April 1878, Edison traveled to Washington to demonstrate the phonograph before the **National Academy of Sciences**, members of Congress, and President Rutherford B. Hayes. The *Washington Post* described the inventor as a "genius" and his presentation as "a scene . . . that will live in history."

It was around this time that people started calling Edison "the wizard of Menlo Park," not knowing that his biggest invention was still ahead of him.

Edison was already hard at work, figuring out a way to use electricity as a light source. At that time, homes, factories, and offices were lit by one of three things: candles, oil lamps, or gas lamps. Each of these was dangerous and could cause fires. Gas also smelled bad, gave people headaches, and dirtied the walls of rooms.

As Edison and his team dove into the electric lighting project, they quickly discovered that the best way to contain the electrical current was to surround it with glass—in a bulb. Then they decided they needed to remove all the oxygen from the bulb; they used a vacuum pump for that. Last, they had to come up with something to put into the bulb that would burn bright and last for a long time as the current passed through it.

The Menlo Park men tested thousands of materials for this **filament**, including every plant and metal you can think of. They even tried spider webs and human hair. In the end, the material that worked the best was a simple one: cotton thread coated with copper.

On October 22, 1879, Edison turned on the first light bulb, which glowed for more than thirteen hours. Three months later, he figured out how to light up the Menlo Park complex for Christmas. Soon he was working on plans to bring electric light to big cities, starting with the financial district in New York City. (He knew how to impress his investors!)

In the middle of all this, his biggest success, tragedy struck Thomas Edison. His wife Mary died, leaving him alone to raise their three young children.

It took some time, but Edison finally found someone new to love. Mina Miller was the daughter of an inventor, so she understood the life her fiancé led. The couple was married in 1886, and they moved with his children to a new home in West Orange, New Jersey. They would later have three more children of their own.

Edison also moved his invention factory to West Orange, where he built a new complex that was ten times bigger than the one in Menlo Park. He hired more people to develop his ideas, but he continued to work as hard as ever. (It was said he could get by on just two hours of sleep a night.)

In the 1880s, Edison moved from inventions involving sound to those involving pictures—motion pictures. He designed a machine that recorded images and one that projected them. Not only that, he built the first movie studio in America. Most of the movies made there were very short—around thirty seconds or so—and captured such things as athletic events and acrobats. A famous American director named Edwin S. Porter credited Edison with giving him his start in the business.

At least one Edison employee thought that the inventor stood in his way. Nikola Tesla told the great man that he could improve the electrical motors and generators the factory had developed. According to Tesla, Edison offered to pay him $50,000 if it could be done. When the younger man succeeded, he asked Edison for his money but was told it had all been a joke. Instead, Edison offered to raise his pay. Tesla refused and immediately resigned.

The two met again in the 1890s, when Tesla had joined forces with inventor George Westinghouse to develop a system that would challenge the Edison method of delivering electricity. Edison eventually lost that contest, which became known as the "War of the Currents."

Edison's interest in electricity prompted him to think about how he could improve batteries. He discovered a way to build huge ones to light ships at sea and tiny ones to power the beams on coal miners' helmets.

In the 1920s, Edison started to experiment with plants. With funding from carmaker Henry Ford and tiremaker Harvey Firestone, he tried to find an American source of rubber—the main ingredient in making tires. After much trial and error, he decided that a common herb called goldenrod would do the job.

As Edison grew older, the three men became great friends and vacationed together in Michigan's Upper

Peninsula. Ford also named his Dearborn museum complex for the inventor.

Though Edison never attended college, he was so respected by his peers that he was given membership in the National Academy of Sciences. The next year, 1928, he received the **Congressional Gold Medal** for his 1,093 US **patents**. He appreciated these honors, but he also noted the importance of hard work. "Genius is one percent inspiration," he once said, "and 99 percent perspiration."

On October 18, 1931, Thomas Edison passed away. At 10 p.m. on the evening of his funeral, President Herbert Hoover asked Americans to turn off their lights to honor the man who lit up the world.

Sources

Adkins, Jan. *DK Biography: Thomas Edison*. New York: DK Children, 2009.

Frith, Margaret. *Who Was Thomas Alva Edison?* New York: Grosset & Dunlap, 2005.

"Genius Before Science." *Washington Post,* April 19, 1878.

Israel, Paul. *Edison: A Life of Invention*. New York: John Wiley & Sons, 1998.

Places to Visit

A museum dedicated to Thomas Edison can be found inside the train depot where he once worked, at 510 Edison Parkway in Port Huron. Outside the building is a statue of him as a railroad newsboy.

A second statue—of Edison as a grown man—is on display at Greenfield Village, 20900 Oakwood Boulevard in Dearborn. This depiction is located in the "Edison at Work" district, alongside buildings from the inventor's Menlo Park complex.

In Detroit's Grand Circus Park stands a fountain dedicated to the inventor. Also, three Michigan historical markers honor Edison. One in Mount Clemens and another in Port Huron describe his youth on the railroad. A third in Dearborn talks about how Henry Ford named his museum complex for his friend.

ONE FINAL FACT

Thomas Edison was challenged by hearing problems, stemming from when he was sick with scarlet fever in his first year. By age twelve, he could only hear another person if he or she were shouting.

GERALD FORD

Michigan's Best-Known Boy Scout
(1913–2006)

"Junior" thought that being an Eagle Scout was an honor. Then he was picked for a special assignment at Fort Mackinac.

Gerald Ford Jr. grew up in a loving household in Grand Rapids as the oldest of four sons. He was a smart boy and athletic, but he had a terrible temper that sometimes got him into trouble. To break him of this habit, his mother, Dorothy, made him recite Rudyard Kipling's poem "If" line by line until he calmed down. It usually worked!

As "Junior" headed into his middle school years, his father suggested that he join the Boy Scouts. According to one Ford biographer, "Scouting, with its exercise, inspirational message and clear rules, suited [him] perfectly. He persuaded half a dozen of his buddies to join the troop. Together, they formed a patrol, and they elected Junior their leader."

You can chart Junior's progress through the scouts by the merit badges he received. His first two were for cooking and "firemanship" (building a fire)—skills he had already learned at home. The first summer he went to Boy Scout camp, he also earned badges in swimming, athletics, first aid, and crafts. In the summer of 1927, he really filled up his sash, adding thirteen more badges. The ones for lifesaving and physical development were easy for him. He also learned carpentry and blacksmithing, and civics and scholarship.

He needed twenty-six badges to reach his goal: becoming an "Eagle Scout," the highest rank possible. Besides the ones mentioned above, he qualified for:

- Automobiling
- Bird study
- Handicraft
- Public health
- Forestry
- First aid for animals
- Electricity
- Pioneering
- Personal health
- Craftsmanship
- Camping
- First aid
- Pathfinding
- Bookbinding
- Cycling
- Canoeing

Ford (left) *and a cousin display their day's catch from a dock while vacationing in Wisconsin.*

He earned his final Eagle Scout badge on August 2, 1927, just a few weeks after his fourteenth birthday.

The next year, Junior showed up early at summer camp to take on a new role, as a member of the staff. He was expected to set up tents, make needed repairs around the grounds, and to kill rattlesnakes (!) before the campers arrived. Around this time, he asked everybody to start calling him by the more adult name of "Jerry." He was proud to serve as a role model for the younger boys.

In September, he returned home to start high school at Grand Rapids South, where he also won a spot as center on the football team.

The summer of 1929 was probably his most exciting in scouting. Not only did he repeat his role as a staff member at camp, he also joined a scout group that sailed a seventy-two-foot schooner on Lake Michigan. Then he got a very special invitation in the mail.

Jerry was asked to become a member of the first **honor guard** to patrol the old fort on Mackinac Island and present its history to visitors. Only Eagle Scouts were asked to fill this guard, and only eight young men were chosen from around the state. Jerry was thrilled to represent the Grand Rapids area.

At the beginning of August, he was whisked off to Lansing the meet the other honor guard members and have a picture taken with Governor Fred Green. By nighttime, the teens were in Mackinaw City boarding a boat for the island.

Gerald Ford's elementary school photo shows a confident young boy with a steady gaze.

For a month, the troop camped inside the fort. During their four-hour shifts, they gave tours of the buildings and fired off the fort's cannons. While off duty, they were free to enjoy the natural beauty of the island.

Of course, Jerry did some sightseeing. But he also used his time to run laps around the fort to stay in shape for football season. And he found another Eagle Scout to hike a ball to.

When the honor guard's time was up, the boys traveled back to their hometowns. Afterward, Jerry sent the state park commissioners a letter thanking them for letting him be a part of this special group. Jerry had learned a lot of valuable lessons during his years as a scout, including how to appreciate the opportunities he was given.

When Jerry returned to Grand Rapids South High School that fall, he jumped right into football, earning all-city and all-state honors.

Jerry also did well in his schoolwork, especially history and government, and he was named the most popular senior by his classmates. These factors and his athletic talent helped him win admission to the University of Michigan.

At college, Ford majored in economics and continued to play football. He helped lead the Wolverines to national titles in 1932 and 1933.

After He Turned Twenty

When Jerry Ford finished college, both the Detroit Lions and the Green Bay Packers offered him a contract. But he turned them down to enter law school; he graduated from Yale University in January 1941.

Ford began to practice law in Grand Rapids, and he thought about running for public office. But when the Japanese attacked Pearl Harbor, prompting America to enter **World War II**, he did his patriotic duty. He became a US Navy officer, serving on an aircraft carrier in the Pacific Ocean. He took part in several major battles with the Japanese and won ten **battle stars**.

Four long years went by before the war ended and Ford was allowed to go home. He did his best to pick up where he left off with his legal career in Grand Rapids. He also met and began dating a friend of a friend named Betty Bloomer. The two hit it off well from the start. They married in October 1948, during Ford's successful **campaign** as a Republican for a seat in the US House of Representatives.

The voters in Ford's district sent him back to the House for twelve more two-year terms. He was known as a hard-working and trustworthy person who could reach across the aisle to get things done. (In the House and the Senate, members of the two main political parties sit across the room from each other.)

As Jerry Ford approached the age of sixty, he began to think about retirement. But fate had other plans for him.

In October 1973, Vice President Spiro Agnew resigned after it was proven that he had taken bribes while in office. Knowing that Ford was an honorable man, President Richard Nixon asked him to fill this important position. After consulting with his wife and children, Ford said yes. He was sworn in that December.

Eight months later, Nixon resigned in the midst of an investigation into the **Watergate** scandal. The next day, August 9, 1974, Gerald Ford became the thirty-eighth president of the United States. In his acceptance speech, he vowed, "In all my public and private acts as your president, I expect to follow my instincts of openness and candor with full confidence that honesty is always the best policy."

The new president made one of his most difficult decisions just a month after he took office; he granted the former president a **pardon** for any future crimes he might be accused of. Though Ford was strongly criticized for doing this, he believed it was the only way to restore faith in the government.

Ford achieved success in foreign affairs, ending US involvement in Vietnam, working out a **ceasefire** between Israel and Egypt, and signing important treaties with the Soviet Union. But, with just twenty-eight months in his term of office (instead of the usual forty-eight), he struggled to make progress on the economic troubles he inherited.

This last reason was probably why Ford lost to Jimmy Carter in the 1976 election. Soon after, the former president and first lady left Washington for a new life in California.

In retirement, Ford enjoyed visiting with his four children and their children. He wrote a book about his life. He spoke out about important issues that faced America. And, in 1999, he was honored by the University of Michigan,

Ford (center) *helped lay the cornerstone for his Ann Arbor library at a ceremony in 1979.*

which named its school of public policy for him. That same year, he and his wife together received the **Congressional Gold Medal**.

The news of Ford's death in 2006, at the age of ninety-three, was viewed with great sadness in his home state of Michigan. As a sign of respect, four hundred Eagle Scouts lined the roadway to his burial site.

Sources

Booraem, Hendrik V. *Young Jerry Ford: Athlete and Citizen.* Grand Rapids: Wm. B. Eerdmanns Publishing Company, 2013.

"Gerald R. Ford Biography." Gerald R. Ford Presidential Library and Museum. Accessed December 11, 2016. www.fordlibrarymuseum.gov/grf/fordbiop.asp.

Laackman, Blair H. *Gerald R. Ford's Scouting Years.* Grand Rapids: West Michigan Shores Council 266, 1982.

Stabler, David, and Doogie Horner. *Kid Presidents: True Tales of Childhood from America's Presidents.* Philadelphia: Quirk Books, 2014.

Places to Visit

Gerald Ford is celebrated at his presidential museum, located at 303 Pearl Street NW in Grand Rapids, and at his presidential library at 1000 Beal Avenue in Ann Arbor.

Three Michigan historical markers mention Ford. The first is in Holland at Ottawa Beach (where Ford often vacationed with his parents and brothers). The second is at Battle Creek's Michigan Central railroad depot (which Ford often passed through). The third is on Mackinac Island, outside of the scout barracks near the fort.

The scout barracks is also the site of a metal bust of Ford. Statues of Ford can be found at his presidential museum; the President Ford Field Service Council building and the East Grand Rapids Community Center in the

Grand Rapids area; and on the campuses of the University of Michigan-Ann Arbor and Albion College.

ONE FINAL FACT

Gerald Ford is the only president to have earned the rank of Eagle Scout.

CASEY KASEM

A Determined Deejay
(1932–2014)

*Blessed with a pleasant voice, Casey talked himself
into a job at Detroit's biggest radio station while
still in college.*

Kemal Amin Kasem was born in Detroit on April 27, 1932, into a family of grocers, a common profession for Lebanese immigrants to America. Everybody thought that Kemal would become one, too, but growing up, the young boy had another goal in mind. He wanted to be a shortstop for a Major League Baseball team.

He didn't have the skills to follow that dream. But, at Detroit's Northwestern High School, he found a different way to get into sports; as part of the school's radio club, he got to be an announcer for athletic events. Kemal also picked up a nickname during his teen years: "Casey," based on his last name.

After his 1950 graduation, Casey worked as a **disc jockey** at the radio station of the Detroit public schools. Following a friend's tip, he then gave radio acting a try, voicing young roles on shows like *The Lone Ranger*.

Casey also studied at Wayne State University, majoring in speech education. He gained valuable experience at the campus radio station and even talked the folks in charge of the biggest station in Detroit—WJR—into giving him a fifteen-minute weekly program. The hard-working young man with the pleasant voice was well on his way to a career in radio.

After He Turned Twenty

In 1952, Casey Kasem's plans were put on hold; that's the year he was drafted into the US Army, which was fighting a war in Korea. Kasem was sent to the southern part of that country, where he worked for the Armed Forces Radio and Television Network. He gained good experience there, playing music to boost the spirits of the men who were fighting on the front line.

When he returned to Detroit, Kasem was hired to read the news at radio station WJBK. For a while, he split his time between this job and hosting a kids' TV show—in a clown suit!

In 1954, Kasem finished college and left home to work in radio out of state. His father's death brought him back to Detroit for a time. Being a good son, he stayed to help out

At the height of his career, DJ Casey Kasem could be heard on one thousand radio stations and in thirty countries around the world.

in the family's grocery-store business. Then, in 1963, Kasem moved to California to restart his career as a disc jockey.

To help pay the bills, Kasem also did some **voice acting**. The most famous role he took was that of Shaggy Rogers on the animated TV show *Scooby-Doo, Where Are You!* He voiced Shaggy for many, many years.

Kasem also created and hosted *American Top 40*, a radio show that highlighted the forty most popular songs of the week. He really put his personality into *AT40*, sharing little-known facts about the musicians and accepting requests for songs from his many listeners. "It was my job to show that there is no easy way to success," he once explained, "and that anyone who got even one Top 40 hit deserved a moment in the sun." At its peak, the show was heard on one thousand radio stations and in thirty countries around the world.

The show made Kasem a big celebrity; he even earned a star on the Hollywood Walk of Fame. He used that fame to fight for things he strongly believed in, such as animal rights, the environment, and promoting Arab-American culture. (Among his many activities was arranging meetings to resolve conflicts between Arab Americans and Jewish Americans.)

By the 1990s, his career was winding down. Then the awards came flooding in, including induction into the National Radio Hall of Fame.

In 2004, he turned over the microphone of *American Top 40* to a new host: Ryan Seacrest of *American Idol* fame. Kasem closed out his last program by inviting his listeners to "keep your feet on the ground and keep reaching for the stars"—something he always tried to do.

Sources

"Casey Kasem." Biography. Accessed December 31, 2016, www.biography.com/people/casey-kasem-21378163.

Silarski, Kim. "Casey at the Mike," *Michigan History* 99.4, July/August 2015.

Trounson, Rebecca, "Casey Kasem Dies at 82; Radio Personality Hosted Top 40 Countdown Show," *Los Angeles Times,* June 15, 2014.

ONE FINAL FACT

Kemal "Casey" Kasem was named for Mustafa Kemal Atatürk, the founder of Turkey, whom Casey's father greatly admired.

CHARLES LANGLADE

A Fur Trapper's Friend
(1729–1801?)

*Born at the height of the fur trade, Charles helped
build the family business in Michigan and Wisconsin.*

In the early 1700s, the **Straits of Mackinac** was a place of
rugged beauty—and it was busy! Each summer, thousands
of Native Americans—carrying the pelts of animals they'd
trapped during the winter—made their way to the area.
There they traded with men who could transport the pelts
to faraway France, which owned this part of the continent.
To protect their profitable fur trade at the straits, the French
built a fort and called it Michilimackinac.

At this fort lived a small group of French soldiers as well
as fur traders and their families. One such trader was named
Augustin Langlade. In 1728, he married a widow named
Domitilde, who was a member of the local band of Odawa
Indians. It was a common practice for French colonists

to marry native women. Their children—called **métis**—linked the two cultures in ways that benefited both.

In 1729, the couple welcomed a baby boy named Charles.

In the wilderness of Michilimackinac, there was no school for Charles to attend. But he was educated by the fort's priest and may also have been sent east to Montreal in Canada for more learning. (Many children of French heritage were.) The young métis was also schooled in the ways of his mother's people.

When Charles was ten years old, his uncle, an Odawa chief named Nissowaquet, had a dream in which the boy appeared as a protecting spirit. Nissowaquet convinced the Langlades to let him take Charles to Tennessee—the home of their enemy, the Chickasaw. The Odawa had lost twice before to this tribe. But the third battle—the one that Charles witnessed—was fought to a draw, followed by a peace treaty. This adventure earned the boy the impressive name of Aukewingeketawso—"defender of his country."

During the next few years, Charles worked with his father in the fur trade. In 1745 or '46, the two canoed down from Michilimackinac and across Lake Michigan to set up a trading post at what is now Green Bay, Wisconsin. From their post, they supplied fur trappers with the goods they needed in the woods: iron ax-heads, kettles to cook in, shirts and blankets, and guns. Charles became a partner in the business as a teenager, and he was known to be fair and honorable.

The Langlades spent their winters in Green Bay and returned to Michilimackinac each summer. While at the fort in 1748, they learned of trouble brewing between the French and the British in an area known as the Ohio Valley.

Ohio was in French territory, but that didn't stop the British from wanting to move their people there and cash in on the fur trade. They were willing to fight for that right, and they began by trying to talk the Ohio Indian tribes into joining them.

After He Turned Twenty

Charles Langlade didn't like what he was hearing. Because of his background, he felt strongly that native tribes should continue to support the French. After all, the two cultures were allies and had built an empire together in North America. Frustrated that his way of life might be destroyed, he joined the French colonial troops.

Langlade saw his first action in 1752. That's when he led a group of about 250 Odawa, Ojibwe, and Potawatomi to punish a band of Miami Indians at Pickawillany for breaking their agreement with the French king. Attacking when most of the men were away hunting, Langlade's warriors forced the remaining residents and British traders they found there to surrender. They then set fire to the village and a British fort nearby. As a result, the Miamis and other tribes in the area once again sided with the French. The colonial governor praised Langlade's leadership in Ohio: "He is [said] to be very brave, to have much influence on the minds of the Indians."

After his victory at Pickawillany, Langlade was asked to take on new responsibilities as an Indian agent, working with area tribes on behalf of the government.

In 1754, Langlade married Charlotte Bourassa, a Michilimackinac trader's daughter. But their honeymoon would prove to be short; that was the same year that bad feelings between the French and British boiled over into what was called the **French and Indian War**.

Early in the war, Langlade was promoted to **ensign** and ordered to Pennsylvania to help defend Fort Duquesne (on the site of modern-day Pittsburgh). The French and Indians were outnumbered by the British troops, but they gained an advantage by hiding behind a ridge of trees and shooting down at the redcoats as they crossed a river. The British suffered many casualties in the battle and retreated so fast that they left their supplies behind.

In 1757, Langlade and his Indian troops traveled farther east, to New York, to defeat Robert Rogers and his rangers at the Battle on Snowshoes. Langlade also took part in the siege of Fort William Henry, where he played an important role in capturing a fleet of British ships.

In honor of his service, the colonial governor made Langlade second in command of the fort at Michilimackinac. Two years would pass before he would be called back into action in the east.

While waiting for that call, Langlade canoed down the east coast of Lake Michigan to set up a trading post at the mouth of the Grand River (where Grand Haven is now

No known painting of Charles Langlade exists, but this likeness was sculpted after his death by one of his descendants.

located). He made friends with Odawa trappers there as well as members of the Potawatomi tribe who lived in the area.

In 1759, the most fateful battle of the French and Indian War was fought; Langlade, leading his men, ended up on the losing side at the Plains of Abraham in Quebec City. The following year, he was made a lieutenant. But the war—and France's control of North America—was lost. He commanded the French force at Michilimackinac until British troops arrived in 1761 to take it over.

Langlade soon realized that if he hoped to keep his trading business, he had to switch his loyalty to Great Britain.

Because he did, he was also allowed to keep his home inside the fort's walls.

In 1763, he began to hear rumors of an **uprising** that the Indian leader Pontiac was planning in the Great Lakes region. Langlade warned George Etherington, British commander of Michilimackinac, of the threat, but the military man unwisely chose not to listen. On June 2, a group of Ojibwe pretended to play baggataway (a game like lacrosse) outside the fort. After tossing the ball over the wall, they slipped inside the gate to retrieve it, then proceeded to kill most of the British soldiers and traders they found. At great risk to himself, Langlade was able to save Etherington and another officer before they were burned at the stake. He also used his influence to gain safe passage away from the straits for prisoners taken during the massacre. Within a year, the British recovered the fort.

In the 1770s, he returned to military duty; this time, he fought for the British against the American colonists. He gathered and led Indian forces at battles stretching from Montreal to Missouri. But the Brits still lost the war.

After it was over, Langlade moved permanently to Green Bay and enjoyed the company of his wife, three children, and old friends. It is said he enjoyed telling tales about the many battles he fought in—ninety-nine, by his count. A companion of Langlade's later said that he "never saw so perfectly cool and fearless a man on the field of battle."

Sources

Plain, David D. *From Ouisconsin to Caughnawaga: Or Tales of the Great Lakes First Nations*. Bloomington, Indiana: Trafford Publishing, 2013.

Trap, Paul. "Mouet de Langlade, Charles-Michel," in *Dictionary of Canadian Biography*. Toronto: University of Toronto/Université Laval 2003.

Widder, Keith R. *Beyond Pontiac's Shadow: Michilimackinac and the Anglo-Indian War of 1763*. East Lansing: Michigan State University Press, 2013.

Zipperer, Sandra J. "Sieur Charles Michel de Langlade: Lost Cause, Lost Culture." *Voyageur* 15.2, Winter/Spring 1999.

Places to Visit

Michilimackinac, the French/British fort where Langlade was born, has been recreated by Mackinac State Historic Parks on the site where it once stood. It can be visited at 102 W. Straits Avenue in Mackinaw City.

ONE FINAL FACT

As a child, Charles learned to speak both French and Odawa, which helped him succeed as a fur trader, soldier, and Indian agent.

JOHN LAUTNER

Born to Build
(1911–1994)

*John developed an eye for architecture when his father
asked him to help construct the family cabin.*

John Lautner was born in one of the most beautiful parts
of Michigan—the city of Marquette on the shores of Lake
Superior. While growing up, he spent as much time as he
could outdoors: swimming and boating in the summer-
time, skiing and playing hockey in the winter, and walking the woods that surrounded his Upper Peninsula city. "I
loved being close to nature," he recalled.

He discovered at the age of twelve that he also loved
to work with his hands. That was the year his father, John
Sr., asked him to help build a cabin in the style of a **chalet**.
(The chalet was designed by his mother, Vida, an artist.)

The building site was a big challenge; it was set up high
on a peninsula that jutted out into the lake. There were only
two ways to get there: by water or by a footpath through

At age twelve, John Lautner (right) *helped his father build a chalet out of logs near their home in Marquette.*

the woods. But the beauty of the location convinced the couple that this was where the chalet had to be.

John and his dad labored side by side for four summers to complete their task, using traditional building methods. "We rafted spruce logs [out to the site]," Lautner explained. "Then he built a **windlass** that had a long arm on it, like you see in pictures of the construction of the Egyptian pyramids. And I ran that windlass, pulling material up the mountainside to build with."

After the logs were hoisted up to the site, father and son trimmed them to size with handsaws and joined them together with rough mortar. They built balconies off the upper floor of the two-story structure and a terrace on the first floor. All of this wood rested on a foundation of field stones, which the pair cut and fit together like a jigsaw puzzle. No part of this project was quick or easy, but John kept up with his father and even offered his own suggestions from time to time.

By 1927, the family of four (now including John's younger sister, Cathleen) was able to move in and enjoy their summers there.

John was a very curious boy. During the school year, he busied himself by reading about every subject under the sun. "I used to go back and forth to the library with ten or fifteen books every week," he said. His world was also expanded by trips to the East Coast when his father—a college professor—took a **sabbatical**. One sabbatical landed the family in Boston and another took them to New York City, where John was awed by the architecture. "Once we visited the Woolworth Building—then the tallest building in the world," he recalled. Working inside were fifteen thousand people, "the same number as the entire population of Marquette!"

At eighteen, John enrolled where his father worked—the Northern State Teachers College (now Northern Michigan University). The teenager had a wide range of interests, and took courses in the arts as well as astronomy, physics, and chemistry. But it was in his father's classroom that he really figured out what he wanted to be. "In sociology, he taught that food, clothing, and shelter were basic to life," he explained. "And I thought, 'Great! I can be an architect, working on one of the basic human needs and contributing to society.'"

After He Turned Twenty

John Lautner graduated with a **bachelor's degree** in 1933. He thought he'd like to hitchhike around Europe for a while, but his mother came up with another idea. She had read about a famous architect named Frank Lloyd Wright who was starting an **apprenticeship** program at his studio in Wisconsin. Lautner applied to join the program and was accepted. He soon moved there along with his fiancée Mary Roberts.

Lautner was a popular athlete and student leader at Graveraet High School.

Being an apprentice was exactly what Lautner needed to gain more experience for his career. Like everyone else, he helped in the drafting room, putting Wright's ideas on paper. But he and his fellow students were also encouraged by the architect to develop their own style, "to find our own architecture, and practice it to suit the geography and climate of wherever we ended up. [Nothing was ever] to be repeated or routine." Lautner really took that advice to heart.

Lautner was very good at working with building materials, a talent he had developed while helping his father with their chalet. So Wright put him to work supervising construction at sites in Michigan, Minnesota, Wisconsin, and faraway California. It was to California that Lautner eventually returned when he decided to start his own architectural studio in 1938.

In 1939, Lautner designed his first important building: his own home! It was featured in the magazine *House Beautiful* and praised by architectural critic Henry-Russell Hitchcock as "the best house in the United States by an architect under thirty." (It was also the place that Lautner's four children called home.)

As his reputation grew, Lautner was hired to develop plans for a hotel, a school, a car dealership, and a movie studio. In the late 1940s, he designed a coffee shop in a futuristic style that influenced the look of motels, restaurants, and gas stations for the next twenty years.

In the 1960s, Lautner focused on designing homes that were big and bold. One was even set on a hillside that had a forty-five-degree slope. Lautner solved the problem of this unusual site by putting the entire house on top of a three-story concrete pillar! The pillar pushed the project over budget, and the owner had to find more money to finish it. The Chem Seal Corporation of America, whose materials were used to build the home, bailed him out but asked for one thing in return: the freedom to name it. Over the years, the "Chemosphere" house has become a local landmark and a favorite movie location.

As Lautner moved from one assignment to another, he kept in mind what his **mentor** had told him: "Never repeat yourself."

Lautner liked to work with wood and stone, and he used lots of glass to bring the outside into a building. (His love of nature, formed in the Upper Peninsula, never left him.) But the details of each house were different, depending on the owners' wishes and the location. For example, the Elrod House was built around boulders that rose up into the living room. The Hope House had a soaring roof that looked like birds' wings. And set into the roof of the Sheats-Goldstein House were seven hundred drinking glasses that acted as tiny skylights. But it was the MarVista House that really made people's jaws drop. This huge house overlooking the Pacific Ocean featured a "sky moat": a single-lane swimming pool that circled the building on a terrace.

*Lautner set up his architecture firm
in Los Angeles, California, where he
designed many unique houses.*

Lautner thought that MarVista was one of his greatest accomplishments. But he let people know that he planned to keep on working at his craft: "By the time you're seventy or eighty [in this field], you're still just beginning."

Lautner passed away in 1994, after receiving a gold medal for lifetime achievement in architecture. And the city of Los Angeles marked his one hundredth birthday by declaring July 16, 2011, to be "John Lautner Day." But the real celebration of his life was held that year in Marquette, where special exhibits and events brought the community together to admire and appreciate the boy who built a chalet.

Sources

Hess, Alan. *The Architecture of John Lautner*. New York: Rizzoli International Publications, 2003.

Lautner, John. "Responsibility, Infinity, Nature." An oral history conducted by Marlene L. Laskey under the auspices of the Oral History Program, University of California, Los Angeles, 1986.

Matuscak, Melissa. "John Lautner." *Michigan History*, July/August 2012.

Places to Visit

The DeVos Art Museum on the campus of Northern Michigan University and the Marquette Regional History Center at 145 W. Spring Street both contain artifacts relating to John Lautner.

ONE FINAL FACT

Young John was a natural leader, and was voted president of his senior class at Marquette's Graveraet High School.

JOE LOUIS

A Hard-Hitting Kid
(1914–1981)

As a boy growing up during the Great Depression,
he searched for a way to help his family get by.
He found that boxing could pay the bills.

Struggle. That's the best word to sum up what Joseph Louis Barrow had to live through before he even became an adult.

Born in 1914 in rural Alabama, Joe was the seventh child of **sharecroppers** Munroe and Lillie Barrow.

Not much is known about Joe's early childhood. He was shy, he stuttered when he talked, and he spoke very little until about the age of six. During that time, his father was sent to a mental institution, where he later died. That left the family to fend for themselves.

In 1926, shaken up by an encounter with the **Ku Klux Klan**, the Barrows moved north—to Detroit, Michigan. They were part of a migration of blacks who left the South after **World War I** to escape racism and find better job opportunities.

The Barrows moved into a home in the city's Black Bottom neighborhood. For a time, Joe attended a trade school to learn how to make cabinets. Then the **Great Depression** settled in, and Joe's stepfather lost his job. To bring in some money, the teen left school and worked at delivering the fifty-pound blocks of ice that people used to keep their food cold. (There were no refrigerators back then.) He also started to hang out with a rough crowd. To make sure Joe had something better to do with his time, Lillie insisted he take violin lessons.

But Joe had other ideas. A friend had introduced him to the sport of boxing, and he really liked it. It wasn't long before Joe began taking the violin-lesson money to pay for boxing training at a local recreation center. Afraid of what Lillie might say if she found out, he hid his boxing gloves inside his violin case.

Joe made his **amateur** debut as a boxer in early 1932 at age seventeen. He signed up for the fight using just two of his three names. (Legend has it he left off "Barrow" to continue keeping his mother in the dark.) Joe took a lot of hits in that first fight, and though he ended up losing, he learned a lot. He won his next fight, and the one after that, and the one after that. With strength and hard work, he soon became the best boxer at the rec center.

The next rung up on the ladder of success was to compete in a Golden Gloves tournament against the best from

Young Joe Louis lost his first bout, but he learned to never give up in the ring.

around the city. In 1933, Joe won the Detroit championship in the light-heavyweight category but later lost in the Chicago **Golden Gloves** contest. The next year, he won both. A hand injury forced him to miss the New York City competition, but he recovered in time to win the 1934 national amateur light-heavyweight championship—at nineteen years of age.

As an amateur, Joe racked up an impressive record of fifty wins (forty-three of them knockouts) and four losses. His mother couldn't say no to his career choice after that.

After He Turned Twenty

Turning professional meant that Joe Louis could start making money from boxing. Knowing how much that would help his family, he quickly found a manager and fought his first match—which he won by a knockout in the first round. By the end of 1935, the young fighter had beaten two former heavyweight champions and earned $370,000 in prize money along the way. In that year, he also married a secretary named Marva Trotter, who became the mother of two of his children. (During a second marriage later in life, Louis adopted four children.)

Louis was flying high and much loved by African Americans. But whites, who made up a majority of boxing fans, were not used to looking up to blacks as heroes. To overcome this bias, Louis's managers made him follow a set of rules both inside and outside of the ring. These included:

- Never appear in a photo with alcohol
- Never gloat over a fallen opponent
- Never show off your cars, houses, or other belongings
- Live and fight clean

Louis did his best to stay within the rules. As a result, he was praised in white-owned newspapers, though their reporters insisted on giving him a nickname based on his skin color: the "Brown Bomber."

By spring 1936, Louis had won twenty-seven fights and lost none. He began to feel unbeatable, and he started to slack off on his training. Instead of preparing for a fight with former heavyweight champion Max Schmeling, he spent most of his time learning how to play the game of golf. Schmeling, on the other hand, took the match quite seriously. The German boxer studied Louis's style and found a weakness. With this knowledge, Schmeling was able to knock out Louis in the twelfth round of their fight before forty-five thousand people at Yankee Stadium.

Talk about an epic fail! Louis felt humiliated. But the sting of his defeat was softened by the news that James Braddock, the reigning heavyweight champ, had agreed to fight Louis. If the young Detroiter could beat Braddock, he could take that title for himself.

On the night of that fight, June 22, 1937, Braddock surprised his opponent with a right uppercut to the chin that sent him to the canvas in the first round. But Louis got back up and shook it off. The two then traded hard punches for seven more rounds until Louis finally got the best of Braddock, knocking him out cold.

A cheer went up in the stadium! But nowhere was the victory felt more than in America's African American neighborhoods. As author Langston Hughes explained, "Each time Joe Louis won a fight in those depression years, thousands of black Americans . . . would throng out into the streets all across the land to march and cheer and yell and cry. . . . No one else in the United States has ever had such an effect on Negro emotions—or on mine. I marched and cheered and yelled and cried, too."

After the Braddock match, Louis could have rested on his laurels. Instead, he said, "I don't want to be called champ until I whip Max Schmeling." It would take another year before the men would meet again.

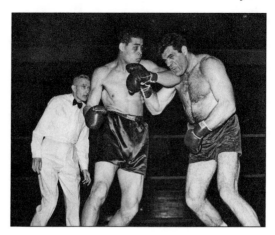

Louis (center) *beat Abe Simon in a 1941 Detroit boxing match, even though Simon outweighed him by fifty pounds.*

They returned to Yankee Stadium for the fight, but this time seventy thousand people turned out to watch. Louis had taken the time to really prepare for this one, and he was in peak physical condition. He also had a strategy: to come out fast, hit hard, and finish the fight in three rounds or less. By two minutes and four seconds into the first round, Louis had knocked Schmeling down three times. For the German's safety, the referee declared the fight over.

For the next three years, Louis took on all comers, defending his title twenty-one times. Then, on December 7, 1941, everything turned upside down; the Japanese bombed Pearl Harbor, an attack that drew America into **World War II**.

The first thing that Louis did was to fight in a charity match to raise money for military families. The next day, on January 10, 1942, he signed up to serve in the army.

Some people criticized Louis for **enlisting**. At the time, the military was separated by race, as many white troops didn't want to serve alongside black troops. Louis's response to them was simple: "Lots of things are wrong with America, but [German dictator Adolph] Hitler ain't going to fix them."

Realizing Louis's potential for boosting morale among the troops, the army sent him around the world. He traveled more than twenty-one thousand miles; his ninety-six fights were seen by two million soldiers.

After the war ended, Joe Louis returned to America to defend his title. But his age had begun to show. In a tough fight with Jersey Joe Walcott, the Detroiter was knocked down twice in the first four rounds. Though Louis still won, he had to admit his skills were failing him. (Most boxers feel this way by the time they turn thirty.)

In 1949, after almost twelve years as the reigning heavyweight champ, Louis stepped away from boxing. Financial problems forced him back into the ring in 1950, but his comeback only lasted one year.

In retirement, Louis tried to stay connected to boxing as a promoter, referee, and advisor to young fighters. He also formed a strong friendship with his old rival Max Schmeling, who visited the former champ often at his Las Vegas home.

The two men probably played golf—Louis's second-favorite sport—during these visits. In 1952, the champ was invited to play in the San Diego Open, becoming the first African American to compete in a professional event. For that, he was later inducted into the National Black Golf Hall of Fame.

In 1982, Joe Louis was honored with the **Congressional Gold Medal** for serving as an enduring "symbol of strength for the nation." He was also among the first athletes elected to the International Boxing Hall of Fame.

Sources

Adler, David A. *Joe Louis: America's Fighter.* Orlando: Gulliver Books, 2005.

Bak, Richard. *Joe Louis: The Great Black Hope.* Boston: Da Capo Press, 1998.

De la Pena, Matt. *The Nation's Hope: The Story of Boxing Legend Joe Louis.* New York: Dial Books for Young Readers, 2011.

"Joe Louis." Box Rec. Accessed December 31, 2016. boxrec. com/media/index.php/Joe_Louis.

Places to Visit

A statue of Joe Louis stands in the lobby of the Cobo Center at 1 Washington Boulevard in Detroit. Nearby, at the corner of Jefferson and Woodward Avenues, is a sculpture of his punching arm and fist.

Louis is mentioned in a Michigan historical marker for Spring Hill Farm, which he owned from 1939 to 1944. The marker is located in River Bends Park in Shelby Township.

ONE FINAL FACT

In Joe's first amateur fight at age seventeen, he wasn't prepared for his opponent's speed. As a result, he was knocked down seven times, but he got up every time.

STEVENS T· MASON

The Boy Governor
(1811–1843)

As a teen, Tom helped his father in the important work
of governing the Michigan Territory.

On October 27, 1811, Stevens Thomson "Tom" Mason was born into one of the most important families in colonial America. His great-grandfather wrote the **constitution** for the state of Virginia, and a grandfather served as a US senator. Tom's own father, John, was a man of big ideas who moved his family from Virginia to Kentucky to seek his fortune.

For a time, the family lived comfortably. John Mason was a lawyer, and he invested his money in ways to increase his income. With his earnings, he bought a large estate and invited important visitors there, including a War of 1812 general named Andrew Jackson. John could also afford to send Tom—then just fifteen—to college at Transylvania University in nearby Lexington.

Transylvania was the most respected school in the area; the sons of the best families went there. Tom took advantage of all that the university offered, studying foreign languages and philosophy.

Then, things started to go wrong at home. John had made some bad business decisions that lost money. To make things easier for his family, Tom agreed to leave Lexington and his chance for a formal education.

Trading his schoolbooks for a shopkeeper's apron, the teenager took a job at a general store. He opened the business each morning, stocked the shelves, and waited on customers. Despite the uncertainty of his future, he carried himself with confidence.

Tom also started to educate himself, reading all he could in his father's personal library. He then got interested in politics and was thrilled when he learned that the man he'd met long ago at his family home had been elected president.

John Mason was excited by Andrew Jackson's news, too, and wrote to ask the great man for a job in the new government. Jackson assigned him to the job of secretary (assistant) to the governor of the Michigan Territory. Leaving the rest of the family behind, John and Tom made their way to the territorial capital—Detroit—in the spring of 1830.

During that period, Detroit was a town on the edge of the frontier, with a population of only 2,200—most of it working class and most belonging to a political party called the **Whigs**. As **Democrats**, the Masons were considered outsiders and unwelcome. To make matters worse, John Mason had trouble pleasing the governor, Lewis Cass.

Son Tom made up for his father's failings. Though only eighteen, he won over many Whigs with his manners and mature attitude. More importantly, he gained the approval of Cass, who gave the teenager a job writing official letters.

It wasn't long before Tom decided to study to become a lawyer.

While Tom was thoroughly enjoying his time in Michigan, his father was not. After just a year on the job, John Mason decided to resign and move on. He told his son to pack up his belongings. The two would travel to Washington, D.C., to deliver the news in person to the president.

Andrew Jackson accepted John's resignation, and even gave him a new assignment in Mexico. After a private meeting with Tom, the president then rewarded the Masons even further; Jackson appointed the teenager to his father's old post and told him to head right back to the territory. The date was July 12, 1831.

When news reached Michigan of the president's action, the Whigs erupted in anger. "Another Democrat," they cried. "And, at 19, this one's not even old enough to vote!" (The voting age at that time was twenty-one.) Making matters worse, Governor Lewis Cass had resigned to take a position in Jackson's **cabinet**. So the Michigan Territory, which stretched from the Detroit River to the western edge of today's Dakotas, would be overseen for a time by a young man who'd had only a year's worth of experience under his belt.

Most people would be a bit nervous about all this responsibility, but not Tom. He looked forward to the challenge. He soothed the ruffled feathers among the Whig leaders by inviting them to meet with him and keeping an open mind about their advice.

After He Turned Twenty

The new governor, George Bryan Porter, arrived in Michigan in September 1831. But he didn't spend much time in the territory. Porter was a native of Pennsylvania, and he frequently returned to his home there. Every time he did this, Mason was left in charge, earning him a nickname: the "Boy Governor."

One of the things that Mason did during Porter's absence was to order the territorial **militia** to march to what is now Wisconsin to drive an Indian chief named Black Hawk and his followers off federal land. Though the settlers' fears about Black Hawk turned out to be unfounded, Mason appeared very strong for taking the step that he did.

In that same year, 1832, Mason asked Congress to declare Michigan a state. When his request was not acted upon, the acting governor called for a census—a head count of all the people who lived in the territory. The count revealed that eighty-six thousand people made their home there—many more than the sixty thousand needed for statehood.

Tom Mason first came to Detroit, capital of the Michigan Territory, when he was nineteen. By the time he was twenty-four, he had become governor.

As the territory celebrated the news, it also mourned a tragedy: Governor Porter, who had returned to Michigan in 1834 during a cholera epidemic, had died from the disease. President Jackson took his time picking a person to replace Porter, so Mason continued on as acting governor.

Then another problem popped up, this one involving land. The Michigan Territory and the state of Ohio both claimed the area around Toledo as their own. The president appointed a committee to settle the argument, but its members could not convince Mason to back down. Not wanting to lose political support in Ohio, Jackson ended up kicking Mason out of office.

By 1835, the voters of the territory were sick and tired of waiting for statehood. So they decided to approve a constitution and elect Mason as governor. Congress refused to recognize either.

By 1836, Mason realized that the only way to statehood was to agree to give the Toledo strip to Ohio. He convinced territorial leaders to accept this loss, but bargained for Michigan to get something in return: the western two-thirds of the Upper Peninsula. This was the deal that finally swayed Congress. On January 26, 1837, its members admitted Michigan to the Union.

In addition to fighting for statehood, Mason felt strongly about education. He developed the first statewide school system, appointed a person to run it, and supported moving the University of Michigan from Detroit to Ann Arbor.

Mason also worked to connect the state with roads, canals, and railroads, but a financial crisis brought a halt to these projects and left the state with a huge debt. Mason traveled to New York City in 1837 to raise money to pay off the debt. Though he didn't succeed at that, Mason did meet a young woman he liked there. He and Julia Phelps were married on November 1, 1838.

When he returned to Detroit with his new bride, Mason found himself taking all the blame for the state's debt. Rather than risk losing in the election of 1839, he decided to retire from politics.

In 1841, the former governor left Michigan for New York to establish a law practice in the big city. He caught pneumonia there in the winter of 1842 and died in January 1843. He was just thirty-one years old.

To this day, Mason is still the youngest person to have served as a governor in the United States. Though his career as a politician ended early, Stevens T. Mason is respected for what he did for the state during his eight years of service. In his honor, the following took his name:

- The city of Mason, Michigan
- Mason County, Michigan
- Mason Hall at Michigan State University in East Lansing
- Mason Hall at the University of Michigan-Ann Arbor
- The Mason Building in Lansing
- Mason Elementary School in Detroit
- Mason Elementary School in Grosse Pointe Woods
- Mason Middle School in Waterford
- Mason Middle and High Schools in Erie
- Mason Middle and High Schools in Mason

Sources

Faber, Don. *The Boy Governor: Stevens T. Mason and the Birth of Michigan Politics.* Ann Arbor: University of Michigan Press, 2012.

"Stevens T. Mason." National Governors Association. Accessed October 23, 2016. www.nga.org/cms/home/ governors/past-governors-bios/page_michigan/col2-content/main-content-list/title_mason_stevens.html.

Weeks, George. *Stewards of the State: The Governors of Michigan*. Lansing: Historical Society of Michigan, 1987.

Places to Visit

A statue and the grave of Stevens T. Mason can be found in Detroit's Capitol Park at the intersection of Grand River Avenue, State Street, and Griswold Street. He is also mentioned on a Michigan historical marker at that site.

ONE FINAL FACT

Young Tom's weakness was a love of fashion. One writer noted that he dressed in "a gleaming silk hat and ruffled opera [cape]" while making his way around the frontier village of Detroit.

WINSOR MCCAY

Kid Cartoonist
(1867?–1934)

He completed his first drawing, of a fire that
destroyed his family home, at the age of four.

Winsor McCay was an extraordinary child who grew up under very ordinary circumstances. He was the first of three children of Robert and Janet McCay, who lived in Spring Lake, Michigan, near Grand Rapids. Robert held many jobs during his life, but he was a grocer when Winsor was born around 1867.

At the time, Spring Lake was in the middle of a business boom. The business was lumber, and many sawmills opened up along the main street to turn rough logs into building planks.

Because these planks were so easy to obtain, nearly the whole town was built with them. Then, one October night in 1871, tragedy struck. A spark from a saw blade started a fire that the townspeople couldn't stop. By the time it burned itself out, most of Spring Lake had been destroyed. Seventy families suddenly became homeless, including the McCays.

Those neighbors whose houses were spared took in the unfortunate families. Crews began right away to rebuild what had been lost, but that awful night was hard to forget. Young Winsor remembered it in great detail, and he amazed his family when he scratched a picture of it onto an ice-covered windowpane. He was only four years old.

Winsor's talent was obvious, but no one knew where it had come from. No one in his family was artistic. And, unfortunately, there was no one in town who could help him develop his skill. The only option left was to teach himself.

He started by drawing as much as he could, whenever he could. "I just couldn't stop drawing, anything and everything," he explained in his later years. "I never cared at all if anyone else liked my drawings, nor did I get discouraged if I made a bad one. I drew on fences, old scraps of paper, slates, [and] sides of barns."

When he was old enough to start school in Spring Lake, he found another surface to draw on: his schoolbooks. Winsor's biographer, John Canemaker, noted that the boy's mother was called in to speak to his teachers about it. She told them it was of little use to punish Winsor for his actions, as "nothing could stop him."

In 1880, another tragedy affected his town and inspired the teen to new heights.

A steamship named the *Alpena* had sailed out of the harbor at nearby Grand Haven with eighty passengers on board. While crossing Lake Michigan, it ran into high winds and huge waves. When last seen by the crew of another ship, the *Alpena* was lying on its side and taking in water.

Three days later, pieces of the ship began to wash ashore. That's when the townspeople knew that it had sunk and no one had survived.

As the adults around him grieved, Winsor—then thirteen years old—began a new project. He drew what he thought the *Alpena* might have looked like just before it slipped beneath the waves. His "canvas" was his classroom's chalkboard and his "pencil" was a piece of chalk. With his teacher's permission, he covered the whole board with the image.

The results were amazing. The other teachers in the school brought their students by to see it. Then people from the town asked if they could look at it, too. Soon, an area photographer came by to take a picture of it. He struck a deal to give Winsor some money for every print of the photo that he sold. Winsor was thrilled with the attention. He could now call himself a working artist.

In his later teens, Winsor took a job at a sawmill, then moved on to a business building wooden boats. He loved the process of fitting pieces together and understanding how every machine in the shop worked. He stayed with this employer until the time came for him to go away to college.

At first, Winsor was excited to go: he wanted to learn more about art. But his father had other plans. As long as Robert was paying, his son would study for a more practical career, in business. When Winsor was nineteen, he grudgingly arrived at Cleary Business College in the southeastern Michigan city of Ypsilanti.

After He Turned Twenty

Being a bit of a rebel, Winsor McCay rarely attended classes. Instead, he would catch the train to Detroit to show off his art skills at a **dime museum**. He drew portraits there for twenty-five cents apiece.

While living in Ypsilanti, McCay met John Goodison, a drawing professor at Michigan State Normal School (now Eastern Michigan University). Goodison offered to give McCay private art lessons, and the young man eagerly accepted. The lessons were practical and focused on such things as learning to draw perspective (with depth) and making the best use of color.

In 1889, McCay left Michigan for Chicago, where he designed circus posters. By 1891, he was living in Cincinnati, Ohio, drawing posters and ads for the Kohl & Middleton dime museum. It was at this museum that he first saw a movie, during a demonstration of Thomas Edison's Vitascope **film projector**. Kohl & Middleton was also where he met his future wife, Maude Dufour.

To increase his income as a newly married man, McCay began working on the side, illustrating stories for

Winsor McCay was a pioneer in comic strips and one of the first people to make his drawings move on film.

newspapers. In 1900, he accepted a position at the *Cincinnati Enquirer* and rose to become head of its art department.

From there, his artistic abilities began to attract attention. When the owner of the *New York Herald* newspaper came calling with a job, McCay jumped at the chance. Working in America's biggest city was an offer he couldn't refuse.

The *Herald* hired him to do editorial cartoons, drawings that drew attention to the serious issues of the day. But McCay was also allowed to develop comic strips to entertain the readers. A popular one, called *Dream of the Rarebit*

Fiend, was aimed at adults. Its characters would have incredible, sometimes terrifying dreams, only to wake up in the last panel, blaming it all on the Welsh rarebit (toasted bread covered in cheese sauce) they had eaten the night before.

In 1905, McCay started a new comic strip that was like *Rarebit Fiend* but drawn for children. He called it *Little Nemo in Slumberland*, and he based the main character on his own little boy, Robert. (He later developed a strip modeled after his daughter, Marion.)

McCay pulled out all the stops for *Little Nemo*. For one thing, each weekly strip took up a whole page. For another, McCay changed the size and shape of the panels to fit the action in the story—like when a forest of mushrooms kept growing and growing. The fantasy worlds that Nemo visited included Jack Frost's ice palace, the Candy Islands, and even the planet Mars—which McCay colored yellow, not red!

In 1906, Winsor McCay was asked to give "chalk talks" (lectures in front of a chalkboard) on the **vaudeville** circuit. McKay was a natural showman, and he amazed the crowds by drawing twenty-five sketches in fifteen minutes. On breaks between performances, he could be found doing his comic strip and editorial work backstage.

As if he weren't busy enough, McCay added yet another arrow to his creative quiver in 1911. That was the year he began to make motion pictures of his cartoons. For his first short film, based on the *Little Nemo* characters, he made four thousand drawings and then sent them to a movie studio to be shot. The result wasn't the first animated film, but it was the best made to that date.

His next movie, *Gertie the Dinosaur*, debuted in 1914 as part of McCay's vaudeville act. The artist introduced Gertie as "the only dinosaur in captivity." Gertie seemed to obey McCay, bowing to the audience and eating a tree and a boulder, though she had a will of her own and sometimes rebelled. In the finale, McCay walked offstage, reappeared in animated form in the film, and had Gertie carry him away.

It was around this time that McCay moved from the *Herald* to the *New York American*—a decision he would soon regret. His boss at the *American* complained that the vaudeville work was cutting into McCay's real work as an editorial cartoonist, and he demanded that his employee give it up. McCay did, but he wasn't happy about it.

The artist continued to produce animated movies for a while longer. In 1921, he released three: *Bug Vaudeville*, in which insects perform on a stage; *The Pet*, featuring a creature with a huge appetite that grows enormously and terrorizes a city; and *The Flying House*, in which a man attaches wings to his house to flee from debt. The public loved his work, which was drawn in the same lush style as his comics. But his employer didn't, so McCay eventually gave up filmmaking, too.

In the remaining years of his career, McCay focused on editorial cartooning. The 1920s and 1930s were a time of turmoil in America, so he had plenty of subjects to work with. The **Great Depression** and **Prohibition** were just two.

McCay was obviously a hard worker and enjoyed robust health most of his life. Despite that, on July 26, 1934, he suffered a fatal stroke. He was in his mid-sixties when he died.

Thankfully, McCay's influence lived on. In 1937, Walt Disney released the world's first full-length animated film, *Snow White and the Seven Dwarfs*, the movie that helped launch his entertainment empire. He graciously gave credit to Winsor McCay as the person who most inspired him.

In the years after McCay's passing, some of his comic strip artwork was lost in a fire. What was saved can now be found in private collections and in museums such as the Smithsonian Institution. His *Little Nemo* and *Gertie* films were also preserved, when the Library of Congress recognized them as important examples of the art of moviemaking.

In a final tribute to this talented Michigan artist, the International Animated Film Society created the Winsor McCay Award. It honors lifetime achievement in the field of animation.

Sources

Canemaker, John. *Winsor McCay: His Life and Art*. New York: Harry N. Abrams, 2005.

Carbaugh, Sam. *Comics: Investigate the History and Technology of American Cartooning*. White River Junction, Vermont: Nomad Press, 2014.

Collier, Kevin Scott. *Growing Up McKay: The Untold Story of Winsor McCay's Life and Times in Spring Lake, Michigan.* Scottsdale: The Book Patch, 2015.

Places to Visit

A Michigan historical marker honors McCay. It is located at 123 East Exchange Street in Spring Lake.

ONE FINAL FACT

Winsor McCay started out in life as "Zenas Winsor McKay." The first two names came from a dear friend of his father. The reason for the change in the spelling of his last name is unknown.

MICHAEL MOORE

Rabble Rouser
(1954–)

*A need to ask "Why?" led eighteen-year-old Michael
to run for a seat on his hometown school board.*

In many ways, Michael Francis Moore was a typical child. He grew up in Davison, Michigan, a small town near Flint, where he spent time riding bikes, playing baseball, and exploring his neighborhood. But he was also a bit advanced for his age.

At his mother's urging, he began reading at the age of four—not from picture books, but from the newspaper. When he entered first grade at St. John's Catholic school, he was way ahead of his peers in his word skills. That sometimes got him in trouble with the nuns, but most appreciated having a child they had to rein in a bit over one who had to constantly be prodded.

Michael was also a very creative child. He had his own pretend TV show at school—complete with a theme song!—and would involve the other kids in it as actors. At another point, he started a newspaper and wrote poems. In eighth grade, he volunteered to write a Christmas play. But when the parish priest saw the dress rehearsal, he decided the show would not go on. Here's why, in Michael's words:

"In the play's key scene, all the nation's rodents held their annual convention in our aging parish hall. [I based this on a bit of reality; when I was] in second grade, a mouse ran up the habit of Sister Ann Joseph—which jolted her out of her chair and had her dancing around to shake the mouse out. So I thought it would be funny to include this."

Father Tomascheski didn't see the humor. Instead of the play, he had the students gather on stage to sing Christmas carols. Michael led a group of boys in silent protest until he locked eyes with a very angry mother superior. "We were all singing by the next song, to be sure," he recalled.

Aside from his spirited antics, Michael also developed a keen awareness of the social issues of the day. A family trip to Washington, D.C., really opened his eyes to this. While there, he got to sit in the galleries of the Senate and House of Representatives as they debated important bills. One bill was intended to protect the voting rights of African Americans. From watching the news on TV, Michael could see that black people were being treated unfairly, and he wondered what he could do to help right this wrong.

The answer came a couple of years later, when his father was thinking about joining the local Elks club. Frank Moore brought home the membership application and asked his son what he thought of the phrase at the top of the page: "Whites Only." "Isn't that illegal?" Michael replied. The answer, in 1970, was "No." Private clubs were still allowed to limit membership to whomever they wanted.

Michael was angered by what he learned. So when he heard that the Elks club was sponsoring a speech contest, he decided to enter it and express his opinion on this policy.

The contest's theme was to honor the life of Abraham Lincoln, but Michael used that as a jumping-off point to criticize the club for rejecting the people that Lincoln had fought so hard to free. His speech caught the attention of the local media; by the end of the evening, CBS News and other national news organizations were calling for interviews.

It took a year of other voices protesting against the Elks club before the group was convinced to open its membership to people of color. Michael learned a valuable lesson from the experience: "That change can occur, and it can occur anywhere." Soon he would lead change on another front, from inside his own school.

During his years at Davison High, he had been a good student and was well-liked by teachers—except for a few who tired of his never-ending (though thought-provoking!) questions. But he just couldn't get along with the assistant principal, whom he felt was a tyrant. The man even carried a big paddle around that he used to hit students who misbehaved. Something, Michael vowed, had to be done.

It was at this time in our history that the voting age was lowered from twenty-one to eighteen. That also meant that older teens could run for public office. The Davison school board had two openings, and Michael was determined to win one of them to see what changes he could bring about.

To drum up support, he went from door to door in his community, handing out a flier that outlined his strengths. And he stenciled his own lawn signs, spending about one hundred dollars on supplies. In the end, it was more than enough to get elected; he ended up as the top vote-getter in a field of eight candidates.

That night, he was told that—at eighteen—he was the youngest person in Michigan to hold office. The next day, he learned he was the youngest person in the *country*. And he hadn't even graduated yet!

He soon settled into his new responsibility. In his first year on the board, many of his suggestions—which included giving students more rights—were passed. And his concerns about how the high school was being run resulted in both the principal and assistant principal resigning.

After He Turned Twenty

Michael Moore started taking classes at the University of Michigan-Flint while still attending school board meetings. However, midway through his term, his relationship with the other members began to break down. He questioned if all of their decisions were legal and, in frustration, even called the county's lawyer to get his opinion. For all the good Moore tried to do, though, he was branded a trouble-maker and ended up losing the next election.

That was fine with him; he wasn't sure he was cut out for public office anyway. All he knew was that he still wanted to keep fighting for what he believed in. He did that by working with his wife, Kathleen Glynn, and several friends to start a newspaper called the *Flint Voice*.

For ten years, he led the newspaper's staff in a kind of journalism called muckraking—seeking out and expos-ing the wrongdoings of people in power. The mayor was an early target, and the police department, too. Then, the town's main employer, General Motors (GM), began laying off people by the thousands and threatening to close facto-ries. (Moore's own father, an autoworker, was in danger of losing his job.)

It didn't seem enough to just write about this topic, not as the town around him was crumbling. So he decided to make a movie. Called *Roger & Me*, it combined footage of Moore as he tried to talk GM chairman Roger Smith into ending the layoffs with stories of those who were already affected by his decision. The 1989 movie, which often used humor to get across its points, was a big hit nationwide. It also started Moore on a whole new career as a **documen-tary** filmmaker.

In the almost thirty years since, Moore has made ten more movies about subjects he cares deeply about, such as the 2008 financial crisis, military conflicts in the Mid-dle East, and America's health-care system. His *Bowling for*

Michael Moore was a class clown in school. But he grew up to be an Oscar-winning film director.

Columbine movie, which focused on gun violence, won an **Oscar** for best documentary feature.

He's asked some hard questions along the way and made more than a few enemies. But that hasn't stopped him in his quest. "I was taught from a very early age that probably the most American thing you can do is to question what's going on and to try to fix things that you see that aren't right," he once explained in an interview. "I believed that as a young person, and I believe that today."

The Library of Congress agrees with Moore's philosophy. In 2013, they placed *Roger & Me* in the National Film Registry, judging it to be "culturally, historically or aesthetically significant" enough to be preserved for future generations to see.

In between film projects, Michael Moore keeps busy producing television shows and writing books. Now a resident of Traverse City, he's used some of his earnings to restore the community's State movie theater and to launch a film festival.

Sources

"Michael Moore." Biography. Accessed October 16, 2016. www.biography.com/people/michael-moore-9542483#synopsis.

Moore, Michael. *Here Comes Trouble: Stories from My Life.* New York: Grand Central Publishing, 2011.

Schultz, Emily. *Michael Moore: A Biography.* Toronto: ECW Publishing, 2005.

ONE FINAL FACT

At Davison High School, Michael was active in drama and debate, which helped him excel at his future career.

RANSOM OLDS

A Mind for Machines
(1864–1950)

By the time he was sixteen, Ranny Olds was working to grow the family business.

The 1860s were a time of great turmoil in America; it was during this period that the North and South fought a war that nearly split the country in two. But the 1860s were also marked by something positive: the births of many of the people who later developed the automobile industry.

One of these people began life in the village of Geneva, Ohio. Ransom Eli Olds, called "Ranny" by his family, was the youngest of five children born to Pliny and Sarah Olds. Pliny was a **machinist** who later took a job at an ironworks in Cleveland. For a time, the family also owned a farm, and it was Ranny's responsibility to take care of the family horse, Old Bess. It didn't take long for Ranny to decide that he hated horses: their smell; their stubborn streak; and the

*As a teen, Ransom Olds juggled his schoolwork with
responsibilities at his family's machine shop.*

time it took to water, feed, and groom them. He thought
to himself that there must be a better way to get around!

As a young teen, Ranny focused his attention on
mechanical things. While walking around the farm one day,
he found a broken-down dam that had once been used to
power a sawmill. It didn't take long for Ranny to figure
out that a mechanical saw could help him with one of his
chores: cutting large tree branches down to size for use in
cooking and heating at the farmhouse. After much hard
work, he got the whole operation running again. When a

weekend of rain threatened to destroy the dam, he rushed out to reinforce it. His father found him there, soaking wet and exhausted. Not knowing how much the repair project had meant to his son, Pliny yelled, "Don't you know better than to work in the rain?" He then gave Ranny a whipping for lacking common sense. But having to go back to hand-sawing wood hurt Ranny even more.

In 1880, Pliny Olds traded his Ohio farm for a house and two lots in Michigan's capital city, Lansing. He then sold the extra lot to buy equipment for a machine shop that he opened later that year.

From the start, Ranny was involved in the business. Each day, he got up at five in the morning to fire up the boiler at the shop, come home, eat breakfast, and hurry off to school. He worked in the shop after class in the afternoons and on Saturdays, eager to learn everything he could about repairing carriages, farm implements, and factory machines. He also took business courses to help his father better manage their money.

In 1883, Ranny started working at the shop full time. And, within two years, he was able to buy into the business. He was proud to be included on a sign outside of the building that read "P. F. Olds & Son."

After He Turned Twenty

In his new role, Ranny (now calling himself "R. E.") Olds worked even harder than before. After the workday was done, he stayed late to record money coming in and going out of the business. Then he would work on his own project: building a self-propelled carriage.

Olds had ridden aboard steam-powered trains and boats, and he thought that this same form of power could be used to make a carriage move. He'd just have to design an engine to do it.

The workers at the shop teased him about his "horseless carriage," and so did the neighbors, who took to calling the young man "that crazy Olds kid." Their comments just made him even more determined to succeed.

In 1887, he did succeed, sort of. Before dawn one day, he made his way out onto the street in a steam-powered, three-wheeled vehicle. But he didn't account for the noise his vehicle would make. It ended up scaring the milkman's horse, which tore off down the street and spilled milk left and right. Then a pack of barking dogs came running up to add to the clamor. At that point, Olds's invention ran out of steam and came to a halt.

While he waited for the boiler to build up more steam, he had to listen to the complaints from the crowd he had attracted. To make matters worse, he had only managed to travel two blocks from the shop.

When he finally got home, his father was waiting for him. It was hard to tell if the older man was proud or frustrated. Finally, Pliny said, "Better get the fires started, then come to breakfast." R. E. did as he was asked, but he was already thinking about how he could make improvements on his creation.

In between tinkering and his work at the shop, Olds did manage to squeeze in time for a social life. On a boat ride, he met a Lansing shopgirl named Metta Woodward. The couple welcomed four children during their long marriage.

In 1892, Olds came up with a better vehicle, this one built on a four-wheel frame. But it wasn't until the young man switched its engine from steam power to gasoline, and was granted the first of his thirty-four **patents**, that he began to draw attention from businessmen willing to support his work. With their money, Olds was able to form a "motor carriage" company in 1897.

Soon, two factories were built: one in Lansing and one in Detroit. Together they turned out Curved Dash Oldsmobiles (named for its front end, designed to keep riders' feet warm) at a rate of twenty a day, using an **assembly line** of Olds's design. The Curved Dash quickly became the most popular car in the country.

Business was booming, but some of Olds's investors got greedy. They figured they could make even more money if the company focused on building expensive cars for the rich. Olds wanted to keep making low-priced, dependable cars for everyone else. When the two sides couldn't agree, Olds decided to leave. He then set up a new company, using his initials—REO—as the name.

The first REO rolled out of a manufacturing plant in Lansing in 1905, and sales were strong for the next few years. In 1910, Olds founded a second company to begin building trucks.

Olds (front seat, left), *then the owner of an automobile company, drove President Theodore Roosevelt in Lansing's fiftieth anniversary parade.*

The following year, R. E. Olds built what he considered his best model: REO the Fifth. "To that," Olds said, "I have added all I have learned in 25 years of continuous striving. So this car, I believe, comes pretty close to finality."

By 1915, Olds had grown tired of both automobiles and trucks and was eager to try something new. Drawing on his deep knowledge of engines, he designed and patented the first gas-powered lawnmower, then formed a company to produce it.

All of these ventures made Olds a wealthy man, and he used much of that wealth to support his community. He created several side businesses to supply his factories with parts. He organized a bank and paid for the construction of the city's first skyscraper. He also donated money to Michigan State University, which enabled the school to erect an engineering building after a devastating fire.

In 1916, R. E. Olds tried his hand at building something completely different: a city! He began by buying thirty-seven thousand acres of land on Florida's Tampa Bay and then hiring a planner to develop a community with wide, tree-lined boulevards; a library; schools; a post office; and a city hall. To attract tourists, Olds also had a casino built with a huge pier jutting out into the bay. Though he invested more than $4 million in the project, it didn't develop as quickly as he'd hoped. He ended up selling the land to others, who eventually grew it into today's community of Oldsmar.

Oldsmar was one of the few projects R. E. Olds failed at. But we remember him today for his successes as a technical genius and smart businessman who showed his competitors how to build an industry.

Sources

Heyden, Patricia E. *Metta and R. E. Olds: Loves, Lives, Labors.* Lansing: Stuart Publishing, 1997.

May, George S. *R. E. Olds: Auto Industry Pioneer.* Grand Rapids: William B. Eerdmans Publishing, 1977.

Walkinshaw, James R. "Ransom Eli Olds." GM Heritage Center. Accessed April 1, 2017. history.gmheritagecenter.com/wiki/index.php/Olds, Ransom_Eli.

Yarnell, Duane. *Auto Pioneering: A Remarkable Story of Ransom E. Olds, Father of Oldsmobile and Reo.* Lansing: Franklin DeKleine Company, 1949.

Places to Visit

A museum dedicated to Ransom Olds can be found at 240 Museum Drive in Lansing. Inside the building is a statue of him welcoming visitors.

Three Michigan historical markers are related to Olds. Two are located in Lansing: one outside the Olds museum and one at the former location of his REO factory at 1445 S. Washington. A third marker has been placed on Casino Way in Detroit's Belle Isle Park. This site is near his Oldsmobile factory.

Olds Hall, the Michigan State University classroom building that Ransom Olds helped finance, is located at 408 W. Circle Drive in East Lansing.

ONE FINAL FACT

From the start, Ransom Olds had a clever mind. He once fixed a broken-down sewing machine and gave it to his mother so she could sew the family's clothing more easily.

SIMON POKAGON

Chief in Training
(1830–1899)

The son of a Potawatomi chief, Simon had
to leave the state to prepare himself to lead.

For about two hundred years, starting in the mid-1600s, the Potawatomi Indians were constantly on the move. Iroquois warriors pushed them out of southern Michigan, forcing them to resettle in northern Michigan and Wisconsin. Then, when they were able to return to their homeland, they discovered Europeans—French missionaries and traders—moving through the area. They befriended the French and fought with them in their battles against the British. When the British won, the Potawatomi accepted their rule, and they later fought by their side against the Americans in the **Revolutionary War**. Ending up on the losing side again, the Potawatomis were forced to sign treaties that took away much of their land.

In the late 1820s, Chief Leopold Pokagon—whose claims stretched around the southern end of Lake Michigan—had to sell a million acres for a fraction of what they were worth. That left him and his people with just 874 acres, near present-day Dowagiac, on which to farm, fish, and hunt.

But the American government didn't stop there. In May 1830, Congress passed the Indian Removal Act, giving them the power to relocate *all* tribes to the other side of the Mississippi River. Leopold thought hard about how to protect his people from another upheaval. He traveled to Detroit that July, to build an alliance with an influential Catholic priest there. Leopold and his family were then baptized into the faith, and they encouraged other members of their band to join them.

It was during this year that a son, Simon, was born to the chief and his wife, Elizabeth.

When Simon was three, a treaty was signed in Chicago that required the Potawatomi to move west—all, that is, except for Leopold's band. The chief's embrace of Christianity had saved his people from this fate.

With the band finally free from threats, Simon could focus on learning traditional Indian ways. He was schooled in the tribal language. He was taught how to live off the land. And he observed the many ways his father demonstrated his leadership.

When Simon was eleven, Leopold passed away. As the youngest of his father's three sons, Simon knew he might

*Simon Pokagon served as chief of a band
of Potawatomis in southwest Michigan and
fought for payment owed to them by the US
government.*

never become chief of the band, but he was still expected to
prepare for leadership by getting a good education. When
the local white schools wouldn't accept him, he got his
mother's permission to travel down the St. Joseph River to
a settlement called South Bend, where a group of priests
were setting up a new school. (This was his first exposure to
formal education; it was also the place he began to master
the English language.) After four years of study, he moved
on to the Bissell Institute of Twinsburg, Ohio. There, in a
setting that brought Indian and white youth together to
learn, he began to develop his writing and speaking skills.

After He Turned Twenty

Simon Pokagon returned to his band in Michigan in 1850. He soon married and made a life for himself in his community. His time to lead would come after the deaths of his two older brothers.

One of his first acts as chief was to figure out a way to get payment for land the band had deeded over to the federal government at the signing of the 1833 Treaty of Chicago. When he couldn't get local officials to listen, Pokagon twice traveled to Washington, D.C., to speak in person to President Abraham Lincoln. In a letter from that time, he wrote: "[Lincoln] is very tall, has a sad face, but he is a good man; I saw it in his eyes and felt it in his hand grasp. He will help us get payment." Pokagon's arguments must have been persuasive; a down payment of almost $40,000 soon arrived, and it was divided evenly among tribe members. (A later payment of more than $100,000 was also received; from that amount, the chief kept only $400 for himself.)

It was around this time that Pokagon suffered a triple tragedy, losing his two children and wife. (He later wrote about them in *Queen of the Woods*, his only novel.) His son had been an alcoholic, and ever afterward, Pokagon promoted **temperance** as a way to save native lives.

In his later years, Simon Pokagon began to serve the Potawatomi in a new way: through his writings. He was a fierce defender of his people and did his best, through articles in national magazines, to explain their plight to white readers. In 1893, he attended the World's Fair in Chicago and was angered that no American Indian had been asked to serve in any official capacity. He was even more disturbed that natives were paid to perform "war dances" every day on the midway of the fair, dishonoring their heritage.

In response, he wrote a booklet called *The Red Man's Rebuke*. In it, he described the city before Europeans arrived as part of a vast hunting ground, filled with many kinds of animals. "We destroyed none, except for food and dress," he explained. "[We] had plenty and were contented and happy." After the white man's wars and westward migration, he said, everything turned bad for his people.

> The remnants of the beasts are now wild and keep beyond the arrow's reach, the fowls fly high in the air, the fish hide themselves in deep waters. We have been driven from the homes of our childhood and from the burial places of our kindred and friends, and scattered far westward into desert places, where multitudes have died from homesickness, cold, and hunger. . . . Our throbbing hearts unceasing say, "The hounds are howling on our tracks."

Pokagon was eventually invited to speak at the fair, to a crowd that numbered in the thousands. In his talk, he explained that his overriding concern was for the long-term welfare of his people: "[They] must be educated and learn the . . . trades of white men . . . [then] they will be able to compete with the dominant race."

Pokagon applied this advice to his own children from his second marriage, encouraging them and his grandchildren to go to school to advance themselves.

At his death, a Chicago newspaper offered this opinion of him: "Gifted with a fine education, and inspired by enlightened views, he was an instrument of far-reaching good to all his people."

Sources

Dickason, David H. "Chief Simon Pokagon: 'The Indian Longfellow.'" *Indiana Magazine of History*, 57.2, June, 1961.

Low, John N. *Imprints: The Pokagon Band of Potawatomi Indians and the City of Chicago*. East Lansing: Michigan State University Press, 2016.

Wiget, Andrew, ed. *Dictionary of Native American Literature*. New York: Garland Publishing, 1994.

Places to Visit

The Simon Pokagon Memorial Research Library is located at 58620 Sink Road in Dowagiac.

ONE FINAL FACT

At the Bissell Institute in Twinsburg, Ohio, Simon became fluent in the classical languages of Latin and Greek.

SAM RAIMI

(1959–)
Middle-School Moviemaker

*With camera in hand, Sam and his friends set out to
make the kinds of movies they wanted to see.*

Back in 1970, dads all across America were buying Kodak's
new Super 8 movie cameras to film the activities of their
growing families. Leonard Raimi of Franklin, Michigan,
was one of those fathers.

His son, Samuel "Sam" Raimi, was excited to see the
camera come into the house. The middle schooler was
already making pocket money as a magician, hiring himself
out to perform at children's birthday parties. He loved the
thrill of surprise that his tricks brought to the audience. "I
could take that surprise to the next level," he thought, "by
making movies to entertain people, too."

Sam talked his brothers Ivan and Ted and a friend
named Bruce Campbell into joining him in his quest. The
three made a series of short films that were inspired by the

Sam Raimi (seated) *discusses a scene with his brother Ivan* (standing left) *and friend Robert Tapert as they make a movie together during their college days.*

slapstick humor they saw in old Three Stooges movies. "Bruce starred in all of them," Sam later explained, "because he was the only good looking one [among us]. 'Girls like you? You go in front of the camera. Girls don't like us? We'll stay behind it.'"

For Sam, the Three Stooges' kind of comedy—with eye poking, hair pulling, face slapping, and pie throwing—was really funny. And getting his friends to do this stuff on camera was funnier still. But he did take moviemaking seriously, too. In fact, he spent time as a teen learning the technical side of the business from a professional in the Detroit area.

After high school, Sam went on to Michigan State University. While there, he helped found a filmmaking club and met another movie lover who would play an important role in his life: Robert Tapert. After three semesters, Sam, Rob, and Bruce began to feel that they already knew enough to make feature-length films (two hours long). So they dropped out, took part-time jobs as waiters, and planned their next move.

They decided that the easiest way to break into the business would be to give horror movies a try. Sam wrote a **screenplay** and figured that the movie would cost $100,000 to make. Then he and his friends began looking for someone to finance it.

To help with their pitch, Sam shot a half-hour trailer. Called *Within the Woods*, it starred Bruce Campbell and three other friends as couples who stir up evil spirits while staying at a cabin in a Michigan forest. To heighten the scariness of a scene when a spirit chases Bruce, Sam screwed the camera to a wooden board and ran after his star with it. There was also a lot of fake stabbing and buckets of fake blood (made out of corn syrup, creamer, and red and blue food coloring).

After He Turned Twenty

The money finally came through for the project, enabling the crew to start shooting the full-length movie—called *The Evil Dead*—in the winter of 1979. Sam Raimi pulled out all the stops for this one, making it even gorier than the trailer. But, despite rave reviews from a local audience, nobody wanted to distribute it.

In 1980, Raimi, Campbell, and Tapert went to New York City to sell the movie, and they had many doors slammed in their faces. Just when they were ready to give up, they met Irvin Shapiro, a producer who was famous for taking chances on unknown filmmakers. He agreed to show the movie at a film festival in France.

There, *The Evil Dead* caught the eye of author Stephen King, who called it "the most ferociously original film of the year." Thanks to King, Raimi's movie finally opened in the United States in 1981, and it became a horror-fan favorite.

The movie's success led Raimi to direct two **sequels**: *Evil Dead II* and *Army of Darkness*. But he didn't want to get stuck in a rut. He fought with Hollywood executives to be able to make other kinds of movies.

In the 1990s, he got his wish: During that decade, he directed a Western, a crime story, a sports drama, and a spooky thriller. Then, at the turn of the twenty-first century, he got the biggest break of his career: an invitation to make a movie about the comic book character Spider-Man.

As a kid, Raimi had loved Spider-Man: a geeky guy who gets bit by a radioactive spider and develops super powers. So he put his heart and soul into the movie. Raimi worked hard to understand the new technology behind special effects. He wanted his audiences to really believe that actor Tobey Maguire could swing from webs and climb

In 2006, Raimi (center) *directed Tobey Maguire and Kirsten Dunst in* Spider-Man 3.

up the sides of buildings. (Among the other actors in the film was Raimi's old friend, Bruce Campbell.)

Raimi had never handled such a big cast and big budget before, and he worried about how well it would all turn out. He didn't have to wait long for an answer; people lined up to buy tickets, making *Spider-Man* the first film in history to earn $100 million on its opening weekend. Later that year, it won the People's Choice Award for "favorite motion picture."

Two *Spider-Man* sequels followed, then Raimi stepped away to do something else. Besides directing, he produced movies and TV shows, wrote scripts for other directors, and even appeared in front of the camera as an actor.

In 2011, he returned to directing with *Oz: The Great and Powerful.* This was another chance for Raimi to grow as a filmmaker. It was his first stab at making a family-friendly movie. (His wife, Gillian Greene, and their five kids appreciated that!) And he got to learn another new technology: filming in 3-D.

Raimi's crew wanted to shoot the film in Canada to save money, but he convinced them otherwise. "If we're not going to shoot in Hollywood, I would really rather do this in Detroit," he told them. "It's my hometown, I can make a much better picture there, and the [crews] are hard-working."

The movie was released in 2013, and once again Raimi hit the ball out of the park. On the strength of the amazing visual and sound effects that he dreamed up—and the performances he got out of James Franco, Mila Kunis, and Michelle Williams—*Oz* made almost half a billion dollars for its studio, Walt Disney Pictures. Raimi made money off the film, too, which he has used ever since to help launch the careers of young filmmakers—people who remind him of himself at that age, with nothing but a head full of ideas and a bucket full of (fake) blood.

Sources

Crow, David. "Sam Raimi: A Retrospective." Den of Geeks. Accessed November 20, 2016. www.denofgeek.com/us/movies/sam-raimi/76599/sam-raimi-a-retrospective.

Muir, John Kenneth. *The Unseen Force: The Films of Sam Raimi*. Montclair, New Jersey: Applause Theatre and Cinema Books, 2004.

"Sam Raimi." Biography. Accessed October 16, 2016. www.biography.com/people/sam-raimi-20716987.

ONE FINAL FACT

When Sam Raimi was twelve, his mother had an artist paint a mural on his bedroom wall. The subject of the mural? Spider-Man!

CLAUDE SHANNON

Top of His Class
(1916–2001)

*Claude graduated from high school early, then earned
two college degrees as he was leaving his teens.*

What makes a genius a genius? For Claude Elwood Shannon, it started with a good education.

Claude was born in Petoskey, Michigan, then grew up in nearby Gaylord. His father was a businessman who encouraged his curious son with gifts like radio kits and **Erector Sets**. His mother was a language teacher and a principal. Even Claude's older sister Catherine played a part in educating him by providing him with math puzzles to solve. (Catherine later became a professor of mathematics.)

Early on, Claude showed an interest in technical things. For fun, he built models of planes, a radio-controlled model boat, and a telegraph system—using barbed-wire fencing—that enabled him to talk to a friend who lived a half-mile away. Claude also worked as a messenger for the Western

Union telegram company. If this last activity sounds familiar, it should. Claude idolized Thomas Edison, who started *his* career in the telegraph industry.

Claude was so smart that he ended up graduating from Gaylord High School at the age of sixteen.

In 1932, he entered the University of Michigan. He had fun there, competing as a gymnast on U-M's team, but mostly he focused on his studies. Taking a double load of classes, he managed to earn two **bachelor's degrees**, in electrical engineering and mathematics, in just four years.

In one of those classes, he was introduced to the mathematical ideas of George Boole. This class proved more important to Claude's career than he could imagine.

After He Turned Twenty

Claude Shannon was full of big ideas. But he knew that if he wanted to be paid for thinking of them, he'd have to get more education. In 1936, he packed up his car and headed for the Massachusetts Institute of Technology (MIT) to study for a **master's degree** in electrical engineering. While there, he was chosen to work with the most advanced computer of the time.

Unlike today's tablets, this computer was big—the size of a room! It was also powered by gears and motors. The more Shannon used the computer, the more he thought it would work better if electrical circuits powered it. (He used Boolean algebra to figure this out.)

This idea was the basis of his thesis—a long paper presenting the results of original research. Because it inspired the design of all future computers, experts have called it the most important thesis of the twentieth century.

In 1941, with his master's and a **doctoral degree** in mathematics in hand, Shannon took a job at Bell Laboratories in New Jersey. America was involved in **World War II** at the time, so all of the lab's researchers worked on military projects. One of Shannon's projects involved cryptography—writing or reading secret messages in code. He was able to prove that it was possible to develop a code that neither man nor machine could break.

Shannon's time at Bell Laboratories was a happy one. He found the work exciting and interesting. And whenever he needed a break, he would ride a unicycle (a one-wheeled bicycle) in the halls, sometimes while juggling.

Claude Shannon left his Gaylord home to enter the University of Michigan, where he joined the math club, the radio club, and the gymnastics team.

At other times, he hopped around on a pogo stick. He loved to tinker and make funny gadgets; among them was a computer, called the THROBAC, that worked only in Roman numerals. While at Bell, he also found time to meet and marry a fellow mathematician named Betty Moore. (The couple ended up having a long life and three children together.)

Unknown to those around him, Shannon was also researching the idea of tying communication and computer science together. In 1948, he published a paper on what was later called "information theory," to much acclaim. His ideas later paved the way for cell phones, e-mail, and the Internet.

In 1958, he was lured back to Massachusetts to become a professor at MIT. He and Betty built a home near the university, complete with a "toy room" that contained more gadgets that he designed—like rocket-powered Frisbees, a flame-throwing trumpet, and foam shoes that made the wearer appear to walk on water.

Shannon thought learning was fun, but he had trouble making it so for his students. He was also terribly shy about speaking in front of people. He eventually asked his **dean** if he could just be paid to research and think. To the mathematician's delight, the answer was yes.

During his later years, Shannon received many awards. The most important was the **National Medal of Science**, which was given to him by President Lyndon Johnson in 1967. Shannon was also recognized for his work by other

Shannon became a professor at the Massachusetts Institute of Technology, teaching at first, then later focusing on research.

countries of the world. For example, Japan honored him with its first Kyoto Prize, given to researchers in fields not covered by the Nobel Prize.

In 1974, the Institute of Electrical and Electronics Engineers created an award, named it after Shannon, and made him the first person to receive it.

Tragically, about the time that Shannon was accepting all of these honors, he began to have problems with his memory. The man who impressed other scientists with his discoveries could suddenly not remember where he parked the car or how to find his way home. His doctors diagnosed him with **Alzheimer's disease**.

In 2001, he was invited back to his hometown of Gaylord to witness the unveiling of a statue created in his honor, but he was too ill to attend. He died later that year.

The genius named Claude Shannon is gone, but definitely not forgotten. The old Bell Labs are now called Shannon Labs. MIT hosts a lecture series named after Shannon each year. And, to celebrate the one hundredth anniversary of Shannon's birth, an international celebration was held that included a scientific conference, a web exhibit, a film, and even a set of **geocaches** placed in Shannon's name in Munich, Germany!

Sources

Brown, Kevin. "Claude Shannon Centennial Celebrants Recall U-M Grad's Advances, Societal Impact." *University Record*, March 8, 2016.

Isaacson, Walter. *The Innovators: How a Group of Hackers, Geniuses, and Geeks Created the Digital Revolution.* New York: Simon & Schuster, 2015.

Soni, Jimmy, and Rob Goodman. *A Mind at Play: How Claude Shannon Invented the Information Age.* New York: Simon & Schuster, 2017.

Places to Visit

The city of Gaylord maintains Claude Shannon Park at 126 W. Main Street. In it is a statue devoted to the scientist. A similar statue can be found inside the Electrical Engineering and Computer Science Building on the North Campus of the University of Michigan–Ann Arbor.

ONE FINAL FACT

Claude Shannon and Thomas Edison were distant cousins. Both were descendants of John Ogden, an important colonial merchant and judge.

GEORGE SIDMAN

Brave in Battle
(1844–1920)

George's desire to inspire his regiment pushed him into
the path of a bullet . . . and into the record books.

Growing up as the son of a bricklayer in the Shiawassee
County community of Owosso, George Sidman might
have thought about following his father into that trade.
Perhaps he'd even begun to train for it. But that would all
change in 1861, when an attack on a faraway fort in South
Carolina marked the beginning of the **Civil War**. Suddenly,
it seemed like everyone was inspired by this terrible act to,
as one recruiting poster put it, "Crush the rebellion! Pre-
serve our glorious union!"

Eager to join his friends, George traveled to the nearby
city of Flint to join the **Union** Army. There he found out
that, at sixteen, he was two years too young to fight. So
he signed on instead as a drummer boy. George spent a
month training with his **regiment**—the 16th Michigan

Infantry—in Detroit. In September 1861, they all moved out, traveling first by steamship then by train to their first assignment: guarding the nation's capital at Washington, D.C.

The regiment set up camp in Arlington, Virginia, for the winter. (Fighting was often suspended during the coldest months of the year.) During that time, George and the other drummer boys learned how to use their instruments to help the commanders during battle. When guns and cannons were being fired, it was hard to hear what the officers were saying. So their orders were passed along by drumbeat. The most impressive was "the long roll"—the signal to attack. One drummer would start a beat, then every other musician in hearing distance would join in until the noise they made sounded like rolling thunder.

George Sidman wasn't very good at drumming; he had trouble remembering the forty or so drumbeats that might be used in combat. As a result, he was ordered to be discharged and sent home.

George was crushed by the news, and begged to be allowed to stay. His request was grudgingly granted, and he was given a musket to carry. He would prove worthy of this weapon the following spring.

In June 1862, George's regiment was marching south with the Union Army's Fifth Corps, hoping to capture the **Confederacy** capital at Richmond, Virginia. Standing in their way were the rebels' best general—Robert E. Lee—and a huge army of fifty-seven thousand men. At a place

George Sidman began his Civil
War career as a drummer boy but
mustered out as a foot soldier.

called Gaines's Mill, the two forces collided. The outnumbered Union soldiers beat back waves of attacks. With daylight fading, though, the Southerners broke through the Fifth Corps' line and sent the Northerners into retreat. During the night, the Union troops escaped across a nearby river and burned the bridges behind them.

During the battle, more than three thousand Northern troops were injured—and George was among them. As he fought off the enemy and encouraged others to do the same, a bullet ripped through his hip. "Dragging himself to an open ditch in the rear, he clubbed his musket over a stump to destroy its usefulness to the enemy, and . . . crawled on his hands and knees off the field," one eyewitness reported.

According to historian Richard Bak, George was then captured by the rebels and later released in a prisoner exchange. Sidman twice fled from hospitals, eager to rejoin his friends. Hobbling along on crutches, then grabbing a ride on a horse-drawn ambulance, Sidman worked his way back to his regiment the best he could. He finally trotted into camp on a broken-down nag he had found by the side of the road.

As one colleague remembered, "Officers and comrades were loud in their approval of his patriotism and faithfulness to duty."

The regiment was involved in two other big battles that summer—at Malvern Hill and Bull Run—and lost twenty of its men. Then, just weeks after his eighteenth birthday, George was wounded a second time. Captain Ziba Graham described the scene:

> Well do I remember that December day in 1862, as we stood en masse on Stafford Heights, overlooking Fredericksburg, all ready to cross the Rappahannock, when the first brigade **colors** for our brigade were brought upon the field. I can see now the eagerness with which this comrade Sidman, a mere boy, with scarce the down of young manhood upon his chin, sprang forward from the ranks and begged of me the permission to carry those colors. It was granted. Colonel Stockton in command, admiring his pluck but [disapproving of] his youth, finally gave his consent. Sidman

brought them out of that hell of fire, many holes shot in them, himself wounded.

This time, George's wound wasn't serious. He was rewarded with a corporal's stripe for his efforts.

Six months later, at the Battle of Middleburg, George found himself in the thick of the fighting again. While charging and driving the enemy from behind stone walls, he was shot in the foot. This was a big problem, as an infantry soldier who can't march isn't much good to his regiment. To give George a chance to heal, his commanding officer had him transferred away from the front line.

After He Turned Twenty

Due to the nature of his injuries, George Sidman was assigned to light duty and—much to his dismay—never had a chance to return to battle. After he was **mustered** out of the Army in November 1865, he returned to Michigan and began to study law. He also married Sarah Lindley, the first of his three wives, who gave birth the following year to a boy named for his father.

During the 1870s, Sidman led quite an adventurous life. He signed on as a member of a whaling-ship crew, then sailed to South Africa to join a diamond- and gold-mining expedition. He was there during the Anglo–Zulu War, and offered to spy on the Zulus for the British government. The Brits rejected his offer, but they did later give him a job in India.

After traveling the world, Sidman settled down to serve in the US Department of the Treasury.

By 1880, he had moved to Washington, D.C., where he took a job with the federal government. As a "special examiner of **pensions**," he worked to make sure that Civil War veterans like him received the proper benefits for their service.

A dozen years passed by. Then, in 1892, Sidman received notice from the government that he would finally be honored for his service at the Battle of Gaines's Mill. In a ceremony in the nation's capital, he was given the Medal of Honor—the military's highest award. The language on his citation made note of his "distinguished bravery in battle" as he rallied his fellow soldiers "to charge a vastly superior force."

George Sidman passed away at the age of seventy-five. He was buried under a simple white headstone at Arlington National Cemetery, which sits on the same ground he made camp at during his first winter at war.

Sources

Bak, Richard. *A Distant Thunder: Michigan in the Civil War*. Ann Arbor: Huron River Press, 2004.

Beyer, Walter F., and Oscar F. Keydel. *Deeds of Valor: How America's Heroes Won the Medal of Honor, Volume 1*. Detroit: The Perrien-Keydel Company, 1901.

"George Dallas Sidman," Congressional Medal of Honor Society. Accessed December 31, 2016. www.cmohs.org/recipient-detail/1246/sidman-george-dallas.php.

Wallace, Lew, et al. *The Story of American Heroism: Thrilling Narratives of Personal Adventures During the Great Civil War, as Told by the Medal Winners and Roll of Honor Men*. Springfield, Ohio: J. W. Jones, 1897.

Places to Visit

Sidman's Medal of Honor can be seen on display in the Civil War gallery at the Michigan Historical Museum, located at 702 W. Kalamazoo Street in Lansing.

ONE FINAL FACT

George Sidman is the youngest Michigan person ever to have received the Medal of Honor.

EDDIE TOLAN

Fleet of Foot
(1908–1967)

*Eddie became a national running star
before he even left high school.*

Thomas Edward "Eddie" Tolan may have been born in Denver, Colorado, but he called Detroit his home. "My father read about better opportunities for Negroes [in Detroit]," Eddie recalled later. "So he packed up Mom and the four kids and we came here."

Eddie arrived at Cass Technical High School on his first day and suddenly felt overwhelmed. It was a huge school—seven stories high—and one that drew talented kids from all over the city. How would he ever fit in? The answer to that question was simple, for him. He had amazing athletic abilities.

In fact, it wasn't long before he had settled into quarterbacking the football team and running for the track team. His body was ideal for a **sprinter**: short (5'6") and compact, with powerful legs that pushed him forward faster at the start of a race than his longer-legged competitors.

His build helped him achieve great things in high school. He loved to run the 100- and 220-yard dashes and was the best in the state in these events for three solid years (1925–1927). He even managed to shave tenths of seconds off his times each year!

In his senior year, he took his talents to a bigger stage: a national track meet where all the best high school athletes went to see just how good they were. More than nine hundred athletes from thirty-six states showed up for the competition. But Eddie was up to the challenge; he easily won both the 100- and 220-yard events.

The next step for Eddie was the University of Michigan, where he hoped to continue his winning ways.

After He Turned Twenty

Eddie Tolan was fortunate to be coached at U-M by two of the greatest sprinters of their generation: Steve Farrell and Charles Hoyt. He soaked up all he could from them, while trying hard to adjust to being one of only two African American athletes on campus.

In his sophomore year, he really started to shine. That's when he broke a Big Ten record and tied the world record for the 100-yard dash with a time of 9.6 seconds.

As a result, the press started to pay attention to him. Much was made in the newspapers about his loose-limbed running style and the fact that he wore glasses. (He couldn't see to run

Eddie Tolan loved football but focused all his efforts on being a sprinter for the University of Michigan track team.

without them, and he worried that they might fly off his face when he was moving, so he taped them to his head!) The other thing that surprised reporters was that Tolan chewed gum while he raced. It helped him calm down and keep a steady pace—right onto the winner's stand.

At the Big Ten championship meet in 1930, Tolan earned his first world record. He took a tenth of a second off his previous year's time in the 100-yard dash. Seven weeks later, he broke the world record in a different event, the 100-meter race, while running uphill! (The finish line was thirty inches higher than the starting point.) In 1931, he ran the same event and broke *his own* record.

After graduation, Tolan enrolled at a teachers' college in hopes of earning a teaching/coaching certificate. He only had a few classes under his belt before he began preparing to run in the 1932 Olympics.

At the Olympic tryouts, it looked like Tolan had met his match: a young man from Illinois named Ralph Metcalfe. The two finished first and second (with Metcalfe in first place), guaranteeing them both a place on the Olympic team. This was the first time that two men of color would be running for the United States in these events.

The press had a field day with this fact, using racial **stereotypes** to describe them. *Los Angeles Times* sports columnist Braven Dyer wrote: "Metcalfe and Tolan make the ace of spades look positively pale by comparison." In other articles, the two men were referred to as the "Sable Cyclones." Metcalfe and Tolan, who roomed together at the games because of their race, pushed these comments aside and focused on doing their best for America.

In front of an enthusiastic crowd in Los Angeles Memorial Stadium, Tolan easily won the 200-meter race, setting an Olympic record with a time of 21.2 seconds. But the 100-meter race was another thing altogether. Metcalfe flew past Tolan in the last seconds, but they both appeared to hit the tape at the finish line in the same moment. It took hours for officials to make a decision about who really won. Finally, Tolan was given the gold, because more of his body leaned over the line.

With those wins, Eddie Tolan became the first man of color in history to earn more than one gold medal at the

Olympics. He also earned the unofficial title of "world's fastest man."

All of Detroit rejoiced at Tolan's performance. When the sprinter came back home, a cheering crowd met him at the train station. And Governor Wilber Brucker declared September 6, 1932, as "Eddie Tolan Day," encouraging cities throughout the state to plan celebrations "as an expression of Michigan's pride in his achievement."

The fame that Tolan experienced was wonderful, but he soon found out that it wouldn't put food on the table. The Olympics were held during the **Great Depression**, and Tolan's whole family was suffering. Like many Detroiters, Tolan's father had lost his job. And his mother was forced to take in other people's laundry to make ends meet. Instead of returning to graduate school, Tolan took their burden upon his back. He looked for a job in Detroit to help out.

It took about a year before he found one, as a clerk to the city's register of deeds. It didn't pay much, but something was better than nothing in those tough times.

Tolan did take a leave of absence in 1934 to travel to Australia to compete in a series of races. He set several Australian records while he was there, and he became the first man to win both the amateur and professional sprint championships. On his way back to the United States, though, he decided it was time to hang up his track shoes.

Tolan continued his work for the city for many years. Then, in the 1960s, he became a health and physical education teacher in the city's elementary schools. No doubt

After his Olympic career was over, Tolan taught health and physical education in Detroit's public schools.

he shared his running philosophy with his young students: "Start fast, run easily, finish strong, and stay in your lane."

Eddie Tolan received many honors in his career, including being named to the Michigan Sports Hall of Fame and the National Track and Field Hall of Fame. But the most important of all may have been when the city of Detroit dedicated a playground to him so that future children would know his name and live by his example.

Sources

Dowdall, Joe. "Olympic Great Tolan Is Dead." *Detroit Free Press*, February 1, 1967.

"Individual Track and Field Champions—1920." Michigan High School Athletic Association. Accessed November 14, 2016. www.mhsaa.com/Sports/Boys-Track-Field/Individual-Champions/1920s.

Sears, Edward S. *Running Through the Ages.* 2nd edition. Jefferson, North Carolina: McFarland, 2015.

Places to Visit

Eddie Tolan's Olympic medals and track shoes can be seen at Detroit's Charles H. Wright Museum of African American History at 315 E. Warren Avenue. Also in Detroit is Tolan Playfield, located at the northwest corner of I-75 and Mack Avenue.

ONE FINAL FACT

Though Eddie excelled at track, his real love was football. He often said that scoring six touchdowns as a quarterback at Cass Tech was his greatest athletic achievement.

JACK WHITE

The Music Maker
(1975–)

*Growing up in a house full of instruments
helped Jack to find his calling.*

There are some advantages to being born into a very big family! John "Jack" Gillis found that out after becoming his parents' tenth child. He wore hand-me-down clothes and had hand-me-down toys, but he also got to play his siblings' old musical instruments, including a set of drums he found in the attic when he was five. That drum set became his first love.

It was about that time that Jack's older brothers introduced him to a singer-songwriter named Bob Dylan. The lyrics (words) Dylan used in his songs were probably too adult for him to understand, but he loved the music, which included folk, blues, and rock and roll. And when Dylan later came to play a concert near Jack's hometown of Detroit, he begged his brothers to take him.

As Jack reached his teen years, his musical education kicked into high gear. At thirteen, he got an acoustic guitar and began jamming with friends. The next year, his father picked up a piano for the family for a hundred dollars. That became the next instrument his young son would master.

By then, Jack wasn't just living *for* music, he was living *with* it! He'd swapped the bed in his room for a small piece of foam, so he could also fit in two drum sets, a tape recorder, three amplifiers, and a stereo. "I really got into drumming along to records," he explained in the documentary *It Might Get Loud.*

After graduating from his parish grade school, Jack set his sights on getting into Detroit's Cass Technical High School. This school drew students from all over the city who were interested in the arts. "I became immersed in art and music and was given plenty of time to work on them," he explained. He ended up playing drums and trombone in the school band.

Though he was busy enough with schoolwork and his music, Jack took on another challenge: at age fifteen, he became an **apprentice** to a local upholsterer (a person who repairs and re-covers old furniture). The older man shared his love of furniture and design with the teen and taught him how to make a living. They would also play music together when the workday was done.

During their jam sessions, Jack discovered new styles of music such as **punk** and **garage rock**. The two even recorded an album together, calling themselves the Upholsterers.

Jack kept working after graduating from Cass Tech in 1993, and he continued his education, too. At Wayne State University, he learned about Orson Welles and a movie he

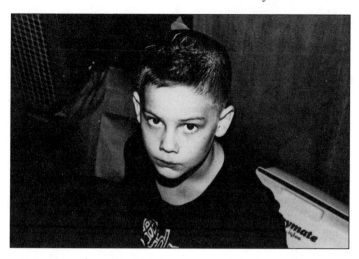

Young Jack grew up in a musical family, and from them learned how to play drums, piano, and guitar.

made called *Citizen Kane*. Jack was in awe of the man's skill at pulling all the parts of the film together—writing the script, hiring the cast and crew, starring in it, and directing it—even though Welles was just in his twenties. The idea of total creative control stuck with the young musician for a long time.

At nineteen, Jack said good-bye to upholstering to take on his first paid gig (musical job), as the drummer for a band called Goober & the Peas. Dressed like old-time country singers but playing with a punk edge, the band taught him a lot about performing on stage. Around this time, he also began dating a woman named Meg White who would play a big role in his early success.

After He Turned Twenty

Goober & the Peas broke up in 1996, freeing Jack Gillis to find another band to play with. That was also the year that he got married. Going against tradition, he decided to take his bride's last name as his own.

In 1997, Jack and Meg made another big decision. They formed a band called the White Stripes, which was a play on their last name and Meg's favorite candies—peppermints. (Peppermints also inspired their clothing, which was always red, white, and black.) Meg White wasn't a natural musician, but she had a way of drumming that sounded good with Jack's high-energy guitar strumming. Two months later, they performed their first show. Within two years, they had written enough songs to record an album.

Music critics really liked their sound, and were amazed at what the couple could do with just two instruments. (Most rock bands have at least three musicians: two guitarists and a drummer.) Thanks to positive press about the White Stripes' work, their fame quickly spread. They began to perform outside of Michigan and even outside the country.

Despite their growing success on stage and in the studio, Jack and Meg White struggled in their marriage. In 2000, they divorced but vowed to continue on as a band.

In 2001, Jack formed his own record label, Third Man Records, so that—like Orson Welles—he could have more control over what he and Meg created. By the time 2003 rolled around, the White Stripes had made four albums. One called *Elephant* won them a **Grammy** award for best alternative music album. And their single "Seven Nation Army" was voted best rock song—a high point in their career.

Another highlight happened in 2007, when Jack and Meg performed in all of Canada's provinces and territories. Just for grins, they ended their tour with a one-note concert in St. John's, Newfoundland. Jack tried hard to get the short performance in the *Guinness Book of World Records*, but the people in charge said no!

The White Stripes made two more albums and won four more Grammys together before calling it quits.

After the split, Jack White moved to Nashville, Tennessee, where he formed several new bands. His first, the Raconteurs, was asked to play as the opening act for Bob Dylan, White's musical idol. It was hard for the young man to contain his excitement! "I have three dads," he declared afterward. "My biological father, God, and Dylan."

During this time, White began to help other artists with their recordings. He also wrote songs for movies and played small roles in several of them.

A big change in his personal life happened in 2005, when he married singer-songwriter Karen Elson. They had two children together, Scarlett and Henry. When Scarlett was six years old, she inspired the song "Sixteen Saltines." As White explained, "I was working on a song and she asked me for a snack. I said, 'What do you want?' And she said, 'I think I'll have 16 saltine crackers.' And I replied, "I think you'll have three!' So she said, 'What about 12?' It was so funny."

White co-founded the White Stripes
and several other bands and has also
gained fame as a solo performer.

Having a family encouraged White to get involved in his adopted community.

He bought a building in downtown Nashville for his label's studio and added a record store and concert space there, too. He also set up a factory to press his albums onto vinyl. When asked why he wanted to use this **vintage** material, White replied, "Vinyl is the real deal. I've always felt like, until you buy the vinyl record, you don't really own the album."

With the turn of the decade, White decided to strike out on his own. A solo album, *Blunderbuss*, came out in 2012 followed by *Lazaretto* in 2014. The recordings each received three Grammy nominations. (As of 2017, White had been nominated thirty-five times and won thirteen of the awards.)

In between those two albums, White heard through friends that the Detroit Masonic Temple—an arts center that he had hung out in as a teen—was in danger of closing because its owners owed more than $100,000 in taxes, so he quietly paid the entire bill. To thank him for the donation, the temple managers renamed one of their theaters for the musician.

More recently, White opened a Third Man Records store, concert space, and album pressing plant in Detroit's Cass Corridor neighborhood. That part of the city, he explained, "has always been the most inspiring area for me." And he shared his hope that today's musicians will work with Third Man Records "to help keep that creative spirit alive for decades to come."

As for Jack White, he's always moving forward: "I have so many projects to work on I'm going to have to live to at least 120 to get some of them done. I'm interested in ideas that can shake us all up."

Sources

Eells, Josh. "Jack Outside the Box: Jack White is the Coolest, Weirdest, Savviest Rock Star of Our Time." *New York Times*, April 5, 2012.

Hasted, Nick. *Jack White: How He Built an Empire from the Blues*. London: Overlook Omnibus, 2016.

"Jack White." All Music. Accessed November 27, 2016. www.allmusic.com/artist/jack-white-mn0000128873/biography.

"Jack White." Biography. Accessed November 27, 2016. www.biography.com/people/jack-white-20631851.

Places to Visit

The Jack White Theater can be found inside Detroit's Masonic Temple, which is located at 500 Temple Street.

ONE FINAL FACT

Before he became a musician, Jack White was in the movies. At age ten, he played an altar boy in the Detroit-made mystery *The Rosary Murders*.

PETER WHITE

A Town Founder
(1830–1908)

Peter served as a sailor, storekeeper,
and prospector before helping to clear land
for the community of Marquette.

Born in 1830 to an Episcopalian minister and his wife, Peter White might have spent a quiet childhood growing up in the farmlands of central New York. But two events changed all that. First, his mother died when he was very young. Then, perhaps in response to that sad event, Mr. White took advantage of the recently opened **Erie Canal** to move himself and Peter to a new home in the Wisconsin Territory.

The trip took the impressionable young boy through a long stretch of Lake Huron, past the wilderness at the tip of the Lower Peninsula, and into Lake Michigan. Father and son then settled in the village of Green Bay, where Peter entered school.

A few years passed, and his father married again. Unhappy at home and at school, Peter chose to leave Green Bay at the age of thirteen, sailing east to the fur-trading and fishing community of Mackinac Island, Michigan. He stayed there for a while, picking up odd jobs and tending a store. But soon he made his way north to Sault Ste. Marie, and from there he hired on to work on a **schooner** sailing between Detroit and the Sault.

During one downbound trip, Peter fell and broke his arm. When he arrived in Detroit, the arm had swelled to a dangerous size, and doctors told him it should be amputated. Luckily, one doctor thought otherwise; he reset the break, allowing it to heal properly.

As soon as he could, Peter shipped out again—this time, finding work building a pier at Waugoshance lighthouse west of Mackinaw City. In the winter, he returned to shopkeeping on Mackinac Island.

In early 1849, a man named Robert Graveraet came to the island looking for **prospectors** to help him find iron ore deposits in the Upper Peninsula. Always ready for adventure, the eighteen-year-old Peter signed on.

Getting there was half the battle! The men sailed up toward the Sault on a steamship and soon faced trouble. In Peter White's words, "The seas rolled mountain high [and] before the steamer had accomplished many miles, a huge wave took off the [lifeboat], swept through the gangways, washed overboard much of the freight from the decks, and alarmed the passengers." The captain quickly turned the ship around and sailed back to the island for repairs and resupply.

Their second try was almost as hard as the first. Though the month was April, there was still ice in the water, and the steamer got stuck; some men got out to try to cut through the jam with saws and axes. After a day of this, the captain backed the ship out and took a different route. Then it started to take on water and nearly sunk. "She would have remained there," said Peter, "if not for the aid of an old fellow . . . who proved to be a ship's carpenter. After we unloaded the boat [on shore] and pumped her out, he found the leak, put in a new plank, and we proceeded on our way."

At the rapids of the St. Marys River, the Graveraet party had to unload their gear, tow it overland, and reload it onto a flat-topped boat called a barge. (A canal at the Sault was still six years in the future.) After eight days of rowing, poling, and sailing the craft, the group finally landed at a sheltered bay on Lake Superior. They rested one night at an Ojibwe camp before making their way twelve miles inland.

Each man was given a backpack and told to put in it what he thought he could manage. Peter unwisely stuffed his with forty pounds of food and tools—twice the weight that everyone else was carrying. "I marched bravely up the hills with it for a distance of two miles, by which time I was about as good as used up," Peter explained. "Graveraet came up, and taking my pack on top of his, a much heavier one, marched on with both, as if mine was [light as] a feather, while I trudged on behind and had hard work to keep up." When they arrived at their destination, they set up camp and soon began looking for signs of iron.

The workdays were long and hard, and the insects didn't help. "[We spent a lot of time] fighting mosquitoes at night and black flies through the day," Peter explained. After two months in the woods, the group returned to the shore with samples of ore that proved the area was worth mining.

On July 10, the men began clearing a site on the bay for a settlement they called Worcester. (They later changed the name to Marquette, to honor the French priest and explorer Jacques Marquette.) Ralph Williams, who wrote the life story of Peter White, claimed that the teen was the first person to cut down a tree. Because of this, Peter is considered one of Marquette's founders, though he was not yet twenty.

In time, more men arrived and more land was cleared for the basic buildings needed in an iron-company town. Peter worked as a steam-boiler fireman (the person who built a fire in a boiler to create steam power), then as a mechanic in a machine shop. He also taught himself how to speak Ojibwe and French, and he was a great help to Graveraet whenever the town leader met with men and women from these groups.

Peter also proved his worth when sick passengers from a visiting schooner passed their disease on to the people of Marquette. After the local doctor became ill, Peter offered to tend to the sick. To make them feel better, he rubbed their aching bodies; to ease their fevers, he bathed them with cool water. After two weeks, they all recovered.

Through actions like these, Peter gained the trust of the important people in the frontier town. In 1850, he was asked to run the iron-company store.

After He Turned Twenty

During the next year, the county of Marquette was organized. Because White was good at keeping records and had a head for numbers, he was elected **county clerk**. And that wasn't the only office he held. By 1857, this energetic young man had recorded deeds for land sales, overseen the post office, collected customs fees, and served in the House of Representatives in Lansing.

That year, White also got married to Ellen Hewitt, the daughter of the president of the local mining company. The couple eventually had six children.

Around this time, White began studying law, which he practiced for ten years. He also lent his own money to help people start businesses, and he later founded the community's first bank.

In 1875, White was elected to the Michigan Senate, where he worked to get a railroad laid between St. Ignace and Marquette. He also wrote a bill to start a college in Marquette. Though the bill didn't pass at that time, White continued fighting for it. He couldn't have been happier when Northern State Normal School (now Northern Michigan University) finally opened its doors in 1899.

Peter White came to Marquette as a runaway child. As an adult, he donated much of his fortune to causes that benefited children.

White had a strong faith life, and he helped to start an Episcopal church in his town. For years, he oversaw its Sunday school program. He also put his money behind two other projects that benefited children. In one case, he convinced the US Congress to turn over an island it owned to the city of Marquette to use as a public park. When the city couldn't afford to make improvements, White paid for a road to the island and set aside money to be spent on the first five years of upkeep.

White's second gift for children was all about reading. In 1872, he paid for a building and donated ten thousand of his own books to start Marquette's first library. In 1904, he and several other citizens paid for a new building when the library outgrew its home.

For all that White did for his adopted city, you could call him "Mr. Marquette." But the state as a whole benefited from his generosity as well. For five years, he served as a regent of the University of Michigan. He lent a hand to the institution in many ways, from starting a scholarship for deserving students to promoting its library to helping to pay for its hospital.

Peter White died in the city he helped found in 1908.

Sources

Brinks, Herbert John. "Peter White: A Career of Business and Politics in an Industrial Frontier Community." Ann Arbor, Michigan: University Microfilms, 1965.

White, Peter. "Reminiscences of Early Settlement," in *History of the Upper Peninsula of Michigan*. Chicago: Western Historical Company, 1883.

Williams, Ralph D. *The Honorable Peter White: A Biographical Sketch of the Lake Superior Iron Country*. Cleveland: Penton Publishing Company, 1907.

Places to Visit

Marquette's Peter White Public Library at 217 N. Front Street and the Marquette Regional History Center at 145 W. Spring Street both contain artifacts relating to White.

ONE FINAL FACT

Peter White strongly believed in education. After quitting school in Green Bay at thirteen, he decided to enroll again when he settled by himself on Mackinac Island.

STEVIE WONDER

A Wonder-ful Musician
(1950–)

*Being different didn't stop him from
being the best he could be.*

Stevland "Stevie" Hardaway Judkins's eyesight problems started early. He was born two months premature in Saginaw, and his eyes hadn't had a chance to fully develop. Then he was put into an incubator, a special baby bed covered with a plastic top, so he wouldn't be exposed to germs. Unfortunately, the oxygen that he received inside the incubator further damaged his eyes. By the time he left the hospital fifty-four days later, his parents knew that he would never be able to see.

And that was just one of the challenges Stevie had to face in his childhood. Another was that his father, Calvin, was abusive, and often left the family to fend for itself without any income to depend on.

One good quality that his father had was a love of music, which he passed along to Stevie. Before his son could walk, Calvin bought him a set of bongo drums—an instrument that Stevie played with all day and slept with at night.

In 1953, when Stevie was three, his parents moved him and his two brothers to Detroit. The Judkins family found an apartment on Hastings Street in the heart of an African American neighborhood called Paradise Valley.

Stevie had a terrific time growing up there. He rough-housed with his brothers and got in just as much trouble as they did. His mother, Lula, made a point of not pampering him or limiting him in any way. But when he started talking back to adults at the young age of five, she realized he needed some lessons in respect. That's when she began taking him to church.

He joined the choir at White Stone Baptist, singing with a high, sweet-sounding voice and moving his body to the rhythm of the music. He quickly earned a reputation for being the best thing about the church's services.

As Stevie developed his singing abilities, he also worked hard at learning how to play different instruments. A neighbor who was moving left the boy his piano, his barber gave him a harmonica, and Stevie received a drum kit from the local Lions Club. At eight, he made his professional debut at a concert on Belle Isle. A **disc jockey** who was hosting the show saw Stevie dancing nearby. He asked the boy his name. Stevie told him, then added, "And I can sing and play drums." He was invited up on stage to demonstrate his talents.

As the band started the next song, he sat down at the drum kit, settled into a rhythm, and even threw in a few solos. For his work, he received seventy-five cents.

Around the time he was ten, Stevie started to seek out friends who could expand his musical horizons. One boy, whose mother was friends with Lula, played the guitar—an instrument Stevie hadn't yet mastered—and could also harmonize pretty well. The two put their talents together, calling themselves "Stevie and John," and started jamming on front porches around the neighborhood. Quickly, they found themselves drawing crowds that were three-people deep.

In the music business, it's almost as important who you know as what you know. And John knew somebody pretty big: his cousin Ronnie White, who sang in a popular Detroit group called the Miracles. At John's request, White agreed to listen to the two boys play.

Stevie had decided that rather than playing one of the Miracles' hits, and risk doing a bad job of it, the two boys would instead perform one of their own songs. Actually, it was only part of a song. But it was enough to make White sit up and take notice. He promised the boys he'd come by the next day and take them to the new recording studio that had just opened on West Grand Boulevard. The studio was called **Motown Records**.

With their mothers in tow, the boys toured the studio and performed for one manager, then another one who was higher up the chain. Both men were knocked out

Stevie Wonder amazed the adults around him with his singing, songwriting, and musical skills. The harmonica was one of many instruments that he played.

by Stevie's talent. Eventually, the second man ran upstairs, where Motown owner Berry Gordy had an apartment, burst in the door and shouted, "BG, you've got to come hear this little kid *now!*"

By the end of the day, the duo of Stevie and John was offered a contract. Stevie was just eleven years old. (Because he was so young, he was given a small allowance instead of a salary. The rest of his income went into a bank until his twenty-first birthday.)

Over the next year, John faded into the background, and Stevie was trained as a solo act. Given his age, the staff at the studio took to calling him "little Stevie." How he got the last name "Wonder" is a bit of a mystery. One story says that Motown introduced him as "the eighth wonder of the world" at local talent shows. Whatever the reason for the name change, it stuck. "Little Stevie Wonder" was printed on the covers of his first two albums, both released in 1962.

One of the albums showcased Stevie's mastery of musical instruments. The other had him singing songs made famous by another blind black musician, Ray Charles. Neither recording sold many copies. The studio executives knew they needed to build some buzz around their young performer. So, despite his young age—he was then just twelve—they sent him out on the road with other Motown talents to tour the eastern half of the United States.

The studio booked their performers where they knew they'd find enthusiastic black audiences. They also added a few locations where white teenagers would gather. This was a big gamble during the early 1960s, when many states and cities had laws about keeping people of different races **segregated**.

It didn't matter to Stevie which group he was in front of. He won everybody over with his exciting performances. He did make some of the other singers mad, though; when he was having a good time on stage, he refused to get off, cutting into their time. Once, when a Motown manager dragged him away from the microphone, Stevie cried out, "But look at 'em, listen to 'em," as he pointed to his cheering fans.

It wasn't all fun and games on the tour. While standing outside after a show in Birmingham, Alabama, the Motown performers heard shots ring out. One singer was nearly trampled in the rush to get the whole group on the bus. The driver later found two bullet holes in its side.

When word of Stevie's popularity reached the Motown melody makers back in Detroit, they made a decision: the young teen's next recording would be a "live single" taped during one of his tour performances.

A long song called "Fingertips" was chosen, then split into two parts to fill sides A and B of a **45 record**. It was released in the spring of 1963; by August, it had climbed to the number-one position of *Billboard* magazine's Top 40 chart—only the second Motown hit to get so far.

A live album featuring "Fingertips—Part 1" and "Fingertips—Part 2" along with six other songs was also released that May, and it hit the top of the album chart. No other artist had scored such success with both a single and an album at the same time. Little Stevie Wonder had arrived.

That July, Stevie made his national television debut, performing on a teen-oriented dance show called *American Bandstand*.

As Stevie's popularity rose, he was booked for more and more appearances. As a result, he fell behind in his studies. When his school threatened to make the youngster repeat a grade, his mother and Motown found a special tutor. They also enrolled him in the high school at the Michigan School for the Blind (MSB) in Lansing.

Though considered a **prodigy** because he could learn new instruments with ease, Stevie didn't know much about musical theory, musical history, or other styles of music outside of what he'd been raised on. MSB changed all that. In the school's music department, he was able to learn about these subjects by reading **braille** textbooks and by listening to records of symphony orchestras and operas. He studied classical piano and sang in the school choir. He made friends at the school, and he finally felt accepted for who he was.

Growing up in many ways, he also decided it was time to drop "Little" from his name.

Before he left his teen years, Stevie joined the songwriting department at Motown. Writing lyrics (words) for hits like "The Tears of a Clown," "I Was Made to Love Her," and "Signed, Sealed and Delivered" helped him become a triple-threat talent: a songwriter, singer, and musician.

After He Turned Twenty

In 1970, Stevie married another Motown songwriter named Syreeta Wright. With her support, he really began to branch out on his own. At age twenty-one, he was given the money he'd earned for the past ten years, and he used it to build a home recording studio. He also enrolled in college to study music theory.

When it came time to sign a new contract with Motown, he insisted on some big changes. He won the right to earn more for each record he sold. He also fought for artistic control over his recordings. This gave him the freedom to explore new forms of music that didn't fit the Motown mold, and, for the next twenty years, that's exactly what he did. The music industry must have liked what they heard. They rewarded him with ten **Grammys** during that period.

Wonder experimented with electronic instruments called "synthesizers," and he wrote lyrics that were sometimes playful, sometimes poetic. In 1974, his music became more political. That was the year he released a song called "You Haven't Done Nothin'," which criticized the president at the time, Richard Nixon, and his actions during the **Watergate** scandal.

In 1980, Wonder wrote and recorded a song to support making a national holiday of the birthday of Martin Luther King Jr., a black minister and activist who was killed during the civil rights movement. Wonder also helped King's widow organize a rally in Washington, D.C., and to deliver six million signatures in favor of the holiday to Congress. He backed that up by recording "Ebony and Ivory," with former Beatle Paul McCartney, to encourage people of different races to live in peace together.

In the mid-1980s, Wonder tried something completely different: working on music for movies. It wasn't long before he earned an **Oscar** for best song with "I Just Called to Say I Love You." He also wrote music for director Spike Lee's films.

President Barack Obama placed the Presidential Medal of Freedom around Stevie Wonder's neck at a White House ceremony in 2014.

By the end of the decade, he had been voted into the Rock and Roll Hall of Fame and the one for songwriters. But the honors didn't stop there.

From 1990 to 2010, Stevie Wonder won fifteen more Grammy awards. (His total of twenty-five is the most ever given to a male solo artist.) Some of the Grammys were for his own work and some, like a duet he sang with Beyoncé in 2005, were the work of others. Wonder has also played the harmonica, one of many instruments he's mastered, on dozens of records for other artists.

In 1999, Wonder was named a **Kennedy Center Honoree**. Then, in 2014, President Barack Obama presented him with a **Presidential Medal of Freedom**. Obama called Wonder his "musical hero"—a sentiment shared by millions of people at home and around the world.

On a local level, Milwaukee Avenue, the site of Wonder's first childhood home in Detroit, was recently renamed for the legendary musician.

Sources

Brown, Jeremy K. *Stevie Wonder: Musician.* New York: Chelsea House, 2010.

Gigliotti, Jim. *Who Is Stevie Wonder?* New York: Grosset & Dunlap, 2016.

"Stevie Wonder." Biography. Accessed October 10, 2016. www.biography.com/people/stevie-wonder-9536078#synopsis.

Troupe, Quincy. *Little Stevie Wonder.* Boston: Houghton Mifflin, 2005.

Places to Visit

A monument to Stevie Wonder can be found at the corner of Fulton and N. Sixth Streets in Saginaw, the musician's hometown.

ONE FINAL FACT

Little Stevie's managers at Motown Records were worried about what his voice would sound like when he matured. But as he grew into a **tenor**, he became even more popular!

GLOSSARY

45 record—A vinyl disc that stores music and is played back on a phonograph at forty-five revolutions per minute.

abolitionist—A person who fought to free blacks from slavery. The abolition movement lasted from the 1830s until the Thirteenth Amendment to the US Constitution, making slavery illegal, was ratified in 1865.

Alzheimer's disease—A disease of the brain that causes people to slowly lose their memory and mental abilities as they grow old.

amateur—A person who does something (like a sport) for enjoyment, not payment.

apprentice—A person who works for an experienced person in order to learn a trade.

assembly line—An arrangement of machines, equipment, and workers through which work passes until a finished product is put together.

battle star—A small bronze star worn by servicemen and servicewomen who have fought in battle.

bachelor's degree—A degree given to a student by a college or university after four years of study.

braille—A system of writing for the blind, created by Louis Braille, in which letters are represented by raised dots.

cabinet—A group of people who give advice to the leader of a government.

campaign—The competition of rival candidates.

ceasefire—A temporary end to fighting, as in a war.

chalet—A type of house, with a steep roof that extends past the walls, that is often built in mountainous areas.

Civil War—A defining conflict in American history, fought from 1861 to 1865 between the United States (the Union) and Confederate states that chose to break away and form their own government.

colors—A regimental flag.

Confederacy—A government formed in 1861 by Southern states that withdrew from the United States. A **Confederate** was a soldier or sailor who fought for the Southern side in the Civil War.

Congressional Gold Medal—The highest civilian honor awarded by the legislative branch of the federal government.

constitution—A document that describes the system of beliefs and laws by which a country, state, or organization is governed.

county clerk—The elected official who takes care of documents and business for a county.

dean—A person in charge of a group of departments at a university.

Democrat—A member of a political party formed in 1828 by Andrew Jackson.

dime museum—A lowbrow museum popular during the nineteenth century where such things as wax figures and mythical stuffed creatures were displayed.

disc jockey—A person, also called a deejay or DJ, who plays recorded music on the radio.

doctoral degree—The highest degree that is given by a university.

documentary—A movie or TV program that tells the facts about actual people and events.

earned run average—The average number of earned runs per game scored against a baseball pitcher.

enlist—To volunteer to fight in the military.

ensign—A naval officer of the lowest rank.

Erector Set—A set of miniature metal beams, pulleys, gears, wheels, and electric motors that can be put together and played with.

Erie Canal—A hand-built waterway across the width of New York state that connects the Hudson River to Lake Erie.

extension service—A program where experts travel around an area helping people learn the best way to do work (like farming).

filament—A wire (inside a light bulb) that is made to glow by passing an electrical current through it.

film projector—A machine that displays motion picture film by projecting it onto a screen.

French and Indian War—A North American conflict (1754 to 1763) that was part of a larger world war between Great Britain and France. Also known as the Seven Years' War.

garage rock—An energetic kind of rock music from the 1960s that takes its name from the place most musicians practiced: their parents' garages.

geocache—An outdoor activity in which people use GPS to hide and seek containers around the world.

Golden Gloves—A multitiered competition for amateur boxers that results in a group of national champions.

Grammy—The highest honor in the music industry.

Great Depression—A time during the 1930s when economic problems led to a quarter of all Americans losing their jobs and being unable to find work.

herbarium—A collection of dried plants that botanists can study.

honor guard—A group of Boy Scouts who are asked to serve in a special role, such as adding reverence, dignity, and patriotism to special events.

Kennedy Center Honors—Awards given by the John F. Kennedy Center for the Performing Arts to people who have made important contributions to American culture over their lifetime.

Ku Klux Klan—A secret organization in the United States made up of whites who are opposed to people of other races, religions, and nationalities.

machinist—A tradesperson who makes, assembles, or repairs machinery.

master's degree—A degree that is given after one or two years of special study following a bachelor's degree.

mentor—Someone who teaches or gives help and advice to a less experienced person.

métis—The child of a Native American parent and a white parent, especially one who has French roots.

militia—A group of citizens with some military training that is called to serve in an emergency.

minor leagues—Lower-tier baseball organizations that enable good players to develop their skills.

Motown Records—A Detroit company, started in 1958, that produced music that helped to bridge the racial divide between blacks and whites.

mustered—To be allowed in or out of military service.

National Medal of Science—An honor given by the president of the United States to scientists and engineers who have made important contributions to the advancement of knowledge.

National Academy of Sciences—A society of distinguished scientists that advises the nation's leaders on matters of science and technology.

Oscar—The highest honor in the movie industry, also known as the "Academy Award."

pardon—The act of forgiving a lawbreaker.

patent—An official document that gives a person or company the right to be the only one making or selling a product for a certain period of time.

pennant—The prize that is awarded each year to the champions of Major League Baseball's American League and National League.

pension—A sum paid regularly to a retired person by a former employer or government.

Presidential Medal of Freedom—The highest civilian honor awarded by the executive branch of the federal government.

prodigy—An unusually gifted child.

Prohibition—A period in American history, from 1920 to 1933, when it was illegal to make or sell alcohol.

prospector—A person who searches an area for precious metals, minerals, or oil.

punk rock—An angry kind of rock music from the 1970s, which takes its name from its antisocial lyrics.

regiment—A small army with a special purpose within a larger army—for example, an infantry regiment (soldiers on foot) or a cavalry regiment (soldiers on horseback).

Revolutionary War—An armed conflict (1775–1783) between Great Britain and thirteen of its North American colonies that resulted in the colonists winning their independence.

sabbatical—A period of time during which a teacher does not work at his or her regular job and is able to travel and do research.

schooner—A wind-powered ship with two masts, one large and one small.

screenplay—The written form of a movie that also includes instructions on how it should be acted and filmed.

segregation—The act of keeping one group of people separate from another, especially in terms of race.

sequel—A movie that continues a story begun in another movie.

sharecropper—A farmer who grows crops for a landowner and gets paid some of the money from the sale of the crops.

slapstick humor—Comedy that involves physical action, such as falling down or hitting people.

sprinter—One who runs very fast for a short distance.

stereotype—An unfair or untrue belief that one group holds about another.

Straits of Mackinac—A stretch of water that connects Lake Huron and Lake Michigan and separates the Lower Peninsula from the Upper Peninsula.

temperance—The practice of drinking little or no alcohol.

tenor—The highest adult-male singing voice.

transmitter—A device that sends out radio, television, or telegraph signals.

Union—The Northern side during the Civil War, made up of twenty free states and five slave states that didn't join the Confederacy.

uprising—A local act of defiance against a government.

vaudeville—A lowbrow entertainment popular in the late-nineteenth and early-twentieth centuries that featured a variety of stage acts.

vintage—Something old and valued.

voice acting—To sing or speak in an animated movie or TV show.

Watergate—A 1972 scandal that involved a political crime and cover-up at the Watergate office building in Washington, D.C.

Whig—A member of a political party formed in 1834 to oppose the Democratic Party.

windlass—A machine that hoists or hauls.

World War I—A global conflict, which lasted from 1914 to 1918, between the Allies (France, Great Britain, Russia, Italy, Japan, and the United States) and the Central Powers (Germany, Austria-Hungary, and Turkey). The United States joined the war in 1917.

World War II—A later conflict that pitted the Allies (led by Great Britain, the Soviet Union, the United States, and China) against the Axis countries (led by Germany, Italy, and Japan). WWII lasted from 1939 to 1945; the United States entered the war in 1941.

PHOTO CREDITS

Simon Pokagon: Special Collections Library, University of Michigan.

Sam Raimi: *(young)* Michigan State University Archives and Historical Collections; *(adult)* Newscom.

Claude Shannon: *(young)* Bentley Historical Library, University of Michigan; *(adult)* MIT Museum.

George Sidman: Archives of Michigan.

Eddie Tolan: *(young)* Bentley Historical Library, University of Michigan; *(adult)* Walter P. Reuther Library, Wayne State University.

Jack White: *(young)* Stephen Gillis, Third Man Records; *(adult)* Newscom.

Peter White: Bentley Historical Library, University of Michigan.

Stevie Wonder: *(young)* Detroit Historical Museum; *(adult)* Newscom.